PRAISE FOR MICHAEL ERIC DYSON

"Michael Eric Dyson embodies the ideal public intellectual for our time: translator, boundary-breaker, and healer of a war torn culture."
—Naomi Wolf

"My man Mike Dyson is not only a serious intellectual, but a hip brother who can identify with everyday people."
—Nas

"Effortlessly and with conviction, he weaves together a range of themes from gangsta rap to graduate seminars, deepening them with highly varied and vividly portrayed personal experience."
—Noam Chomsky

"Dyson riffs with speed, eloquence, bawdy humor and startling truths that have the effect of hitting you like a Mack truck."
—*San Francisco Examiner*

"One of the most eloquent and wide-ranging black public intellectuals . . . He moves fluently between academic and popular audiences, between 'high theory' and 'low life.'"
—Stuart Hall

KNOW WHAT I MEAN?

ALSO BY MICHAEL ERIC DYSON

Debating Race (2007)

Pride: The Seven Deadly Sins (2006)

Come Hell or High Water: Hurricane Katrina and the Color of Disaster (2006)

Is Bill Cosby Right? Or Has the Black Middle Class Lost Its Mind? (2005)

Mercy, Mercy Me: The Art, Loves, and Demons of Marvin Gaye (2004)

The Michael Eric Dyson Reader (2004)

Open Mike: Reflections on Philosophy, Race, Sex, Culture, and Religion (2003)

Why I Love Black Women (2003)

Holler If You Hear Me: Searching for Tupac Shakur (2001)

I May Not Get There with You: The True Martin Luther King, Jr. (2000)

Race Rules: Navigating the Color Line (1997)

Between God and Gangsta Rap: Bearing Witness to Black Culture (1996)

Making Malcolm: The Myth and Meaning of Malcolm X (1995)

Reflecting Black: African-American Cultural Criticism (1993)

KNOW WHAT I MEAN?

Reflections on Hip Hop

BY MICHAEL ERIC DYSON

INTRO BY JAY-Z
OUTRO BY NAS

BASIC
CIVITAS
BOOKS

A Member of the Perseus Books Group
New York

Hardcover edition first published in 2007 by Basic Civitas Books,
A Member of the Perseus Books Group
Paperback edition first published in 2010 by Basic Civitas Books

Design by Jane Raese
Text set in 12.5-point Goudy

A CIP catalog record for this book is available from the Library of
Congress.
HC ISBN: 978-0-465-01716-4
PB ISBN: 978-0-465-01807-9

10 9 8 7 6 5 4 3 2 1

TO

SHAWN "JAY Z" CARTER

"A Hustler Disguised as a Rapper"

AND

NASIR "NAS" JONES

"Nas is the Ghetto American Idol"

Two Rhetorical Geniuses
Two of the Greatest Artists of All Time
and
Two Wise Black Men

Who peacefully settled their differences
Joined forces
And changed the game forever

CONTENTS

CONTENTS

INTRO

by Jay-Z

Michael Eric Dyson came up in the tough streets of Detroit. He didn't grow up with silver spoons at the family table. His table didn't have fine china and his path from then to now wasn't clear of trouble and strife. He came up through the church and the world of academia in spite of his experience. Dyson confronted the same disadvantages that afflicted the folks in his neighborhood and that held so many brothers and sisters back. But these circumstances opened his mind to learning, and to a sense of justice that has driven him to succeed. Dyson could have been someone's older brother on my block when I was coming up in the Marcy projects in Bed-Stuy. He could have been the teacher at a Baltimore high school who showed Tupac that there was power in knowledge and your people's history.

Although he wasn't there for either of us then, his preaching and his intellectual actions are there today for countless brothers and sisters, regardless of skin color, and regardless of who they pray to at night. He is there telling everyone who was born into a life that seems destitute and destined for failure that there is a way out. He is there reminding us all not to let our situation be an excuse when it can be a resource. Just as important, he is telling all of those countless people whose minds are closed by bigotry or contempt that hip hop is American. Blackness is American. I am American.

At this point it might seem hollow to repeat what has been widely said about Michael Eric Dyson: this gifted man is the "hip hop intellectual," a world-class scholar, and the most brilliant interpreter of hip hop culture we have. But plain and simple that is what he is. He has shown those doubters and critics that hip hop is a vital arts movement created by young working-class men and women of color. Yes, our rhymes can contain violence and hatred. Yes, our songs can detail the drug business and our choruses can bounce with lustful intent. However, those things did not spring from inferior imaginations or deficient morals; these things came from our lives. They came from America.

The folks from the suburbs and the private schools so concerned with putting warning labels on my records missed the point. They never stopped to worry about the realities in this country that spread poverty and racism and gun violence and hatred of women and drug use and unemployment. People can act like rappers spread these things, but that is not true. Our lives are not rotten or worthless just because that's what people say about the real estate that we were raised on. In fact, our lives may be even more worthy of study because we succeeded despite the promises of failure seeping out from behind the peeling paint on the walls of every apartment in every project.

Dyson came up from the bottom and told those on top what was up. He turned a light on our situation in this country and then he threw down a rope to lift us out. He started out translating between "us" and "them" and now he's helping put together a world where there is only "us." How many folk out there can talk about pimping in terms laid out by Hegel? Or use Kant to explain the way that prison fashion moved from the cellblock to the city block? Dyson drops the names of philosophers and scholars as easily as he does the names of artists on the latest mixtape moving dance floors in the clubs. Michael Eric Dyson has taken modern urban life seriously and brought the tools of so-called legitimate society to bear on a place that too many dismissed as unworthy of attention. Just by mentioning these cats in the same breath he levels a playing field that has always been tilted. He tore down the last "whites only" sign in the university and let all of us rush in to hear what the ancient teachers and scientists had to say.

Dyson stands up for poor folks and for street culture when other African Americans treat us with the same disdain that white society used to have for all of us. He continues to show us what the past can teach us about our present. It's one thing for young people to see rappers making appearances on TRL or to see their records fly up the charts. But it is another thing for a young boy from the hood to go into the library at his school and check out a book on why his culture matters. Quite literally, Dyson has written that book. Money comes and goes, but respect can last for generations. Neither the IRS nor the changing taste of the public can take away what Michael Eric Dyson has given to hip hop: respect and a better way to understand ourselves.

PRELUDE

"WHAT'S BEEF?"

Hip Hop and Its Critics

"Sir, please turn around and face me," the Hartsfield-Jackson airport security employee directed me.

As I complied, he continued to methodically search me at the security checkpoint. This tall, taffy-faced figure barely out of his youth reminded me of my son. As I caught his eye when he frisked my outstretched arms, he whispered to me while maintaining his professional demeanor.

"Man, I really feel your work on Pac," he gently stated, referring to my book *Holler If You Hear Me: Searching for Tupac Shakur*. "Plus, I've seen *Thug Angel* and *Tupac Vs.* [two documentaries on the slain rapper in which I'd participated], and you be puttin' it down."

"May I please place my hands on your chest since my detector went off?" he quizzed me more formally without missing a beat.

"Sure, no problem," I replied. "That's where my suspenders are. And I'm glad you like the work."

"Fo' sho', fo' sho'," he said as he effortlessly slid back into his vernacular voice. "I'm just glad to know that somebody from your generation cares about Pac and hip hop, and takes the time to listen to what we're saying.

"All right sir, I'm finished. You're done. But could you do me a big favor?"

"What's that?" I asked.

The young man retreated to a portable booth tucked away at the end of the security line and fetched a dog-eared paperback copy of my book. His action was all the more remarkable because there was a long line waiting as he handed me my work.

"If you don't mind, please sign this before you go."

I was moved by his heartfelt compliments. He was eloquent proof that not everyone in his generation is illiterate, destructive, and materialistic. We weren't in school, and he wasn't reading my book for extra credit. Like the best students, he read for passion, and for the pleasure and pursuit of intellectual stimulation. He read because he wanted to better understand his life, his world, and why this music mattered to him the way it did. He wanted to find inspired ideas to explain his feelings. Most importantly, he seemed hungry for a sign that intellectuals and older folk understand the importance of hip hop. He also wanted to know that his culture hasn't been blanketed by contempt or smothered by undiscriminating enthusiasm. And his delight in me taking Tupac seriously was an unspoken nod to the fierce crosswinds in which hip hop is presently caught.

There are some, like jazz great Wynton Marsalis, who dismiss hip hop as adolescent "ghetto minstrelsy." Critics like Marsalis see rap as little more than ancient stereotypes wrapped in contemporary rhymes. Other prominent observers, such as social critic Stanley Crouch, claim that the deficits of hip hop blare beyond the borders of ugly art to inspire youth to even uglier behavior. Crouch contends in his column for the *New York Daily News* that hip hop's "elevation of pimps and pimp attitudes creates a sado-masochistic relationship with female fans." It's true that those who fail to wrestle with hip hop's cultural complexity, and approach it in a facile manner, may be misled into unhealthy forms of behavior. But that can be said for all art, including the incest-laden, murder-prone characters sketched in Shakespeare's *Macbeth* and *King Lear*. It makes no sense to stop critically engaging an art form or cultural movement because some kids think it "cool" that 50 Cent got shot nine times.

In fact, that's even more reason to clarify what an art form does well, and what it does poorly. Such balance is woefully lacking in many criticisms of hip hop. For instance, some critics protest that, stripped of politics, history, and racial conscience, hip hop is little more than sonic pathology and all it does is blast away the achievements of the civil rights struggle. But hip hop music is important precisely because it sheds light on contemporary politics, history, and race. At its best, hip hop gives voice to marginal black youth we are not used to hearing from on such topics. Sadly, the enlightened aspects of hip hop are overlooked by critics who are out to satisfy a grudge against black youth culture and are too angry or self-righteous to listen and learn.

Sensational headlines trumpet the moral transgressions or violent deaths of hip hoppers like Tupac Shakur and Jam Master Jay. John McWhorter, a social critic and widely read black conservative author, has made a career of twisting perceived black misbehavior into a provocative, if flawed, analysis of contemporary race. For instance, he lambastes black folk for our victimology and anti-intellectualism in his book *Losing the Race*. McWhorter eloquently weighs in on hip hop culture with lopsided moralizing in New York's *City Journal*. "By reinforcing the stereotypes that long hindered blacks," McWhorter argues, "and by teaching young blacks that a thuggish adversarial stance is the properly 'authentic' response to a presumptively racist society, rap retards black success." The fate of black success is a heavy burden for black youth to carry. That's especially true for the black youth who make a cameo in the anecdote about eight unruly teens who had to be kicked out of a fast food

restaurant that fronts McWhorter's essay. For Mc-
Whorter, these youth embody the "antisocial behavior"
encouraged by hardcore rap that preaches "bone-deep
dislike of authority."

Many critics, including McWhorter, don't account for
the complex ways that some artists in hip hop play with
stereotypes to either subvert or reverse them. Amid the
pimp mythologies and metaphors that gut contemporary
hip hop, rappers like Common—and Xzibit in his wildly
popular MTV series *Pimp My Ride,* devoted to upgrading
broken-down automobiles—seize on pimpology's promi-
nence to poke fun at its pervasiveness. But its critics
often fail to acknowledge that hip hop is neither socio-
logical commentary nor political criticism, though it may
certainly function in these modes through its artists'
lyrics. Hip hop is still fundamentally an *art form* that traf-
fics in hyperbole, parody, kitsch, dramatic license, double
entendres, signification, and other literary and artistic
conventions to get its point across.

By denying its musical and artistic merit, hip hop's
critics get to have it both ways: they can deny the legitimate artistic standing of rap while seizing on its pervasive
influence as an art form to prove what a terrible effect it
has on youth. There are few parallels to this heavy-
handed and wrongheaded approach to the criticism of
other art forms like films, plays, or visual art, especially
when they are authored by nonblacks. These cultural
products are often conceded as art—bad art, useless art,

banal art, but *art* nonetheless. There is far greater consensus about hip hop's essential artlessness. Such cultural bias and unapologetic ignorance reinforce the racial gulfs that fuel rap's resentment of the status quo.

Not all the barbs aimed at hip hop are meant exclusively for its artists. Some are directed at "members of the post–civil rights era generation of Black academics" who matured as writers and intellectuals during the rise of hip hop culture. This group includes scholars like Tricia Rose (author of *Black Noise*), Todd Boyd (*Am I Black Enough for You?*), Mark Anthony Neal (*What the Music Said*), Juan Flores (*From Bomba to Hip Hop*), Murray Forman (*The Hood Comes First*), Cheryl Keyes (*Rap Music and Street Consciousness*), Imani Perry (*Prophets of the Hood*), S. Craig Watkins (*Hip Hop Matters*), Gwendolyn Pough (*Check It While I Wreck It*), Felicia Miyakawa (*Five Percenter Rap*), Kyra Gaunt (*The Games Black Girls Play*), William Jelani Cobb (*To the Break of Dawn*), T. Denean Sharpley-Whiting (*Pimps Up, Ho's Down*), and younger scholars such as James Peterson, Meta DuEwa Jones, Dionne Bennett, Dawn-Elissa Fischer, Kyle Dargan, H. Samy Alim, Rachel Raimist, Scott Heath, Marc Hill, Angie Colette Beatty, and Sohail Daulatzai.

Outside of the academy, there are intellectuals and activists of hip hop and spoken word like Davey D, Rosa Clemente, Byron Hurt (writer/director of the documentary *Hip Hop: Beyond Beats and Rhymes*), Nelson George (*Hip Hop America*), Joan Morgan (*When Chickenheads*

Come Home to Roost), Jessica Care Moore (*The Words Don't Fit in My Mouth*), Bakari Kitwana (*The Hip Hop Generation*), Yvonne Bynoe (*Stand and Deliver*), and Jeff Chang (*Can't Stop Won't Stop*). Revered intellectuals and writers like Crouch, Marsalis, McWhorter, and Martin Kilson, the first African American professor to receive tenure at Harvard, cringe when they think intellectuals who engage hip hop don't embrace the values and styles of earlier arts communities or the civil rights movement.

Kilson accuses the post–civil rights black intelligentsia of "tossing poisoned darts at African Americans' mainline civil rights tradition and its courageous leadership figures." Since he singles me out as a major culprit among "these civil rights tradition–offending" thinkers, I'll presumptuously respond on behalf of an admittedly big and complex group of scholars who, while holding some beliefs in common, also entertain varying, even contradictory views about hip hop culture.

Kilson says that in a September 2002 op-ed for the *New York Times* about the controversial movie *Barbershop*, I claim to belong "to a new generation of Black intellectuals who consider leadership personalities like Martin Luther King Jr. and Rosa Parks fair game for anyone's comedic dishonoring." (I don't make any such claim.) Kilson says I engaged in this practice by defending the "Black people–offending MGM film, *Barbershop*." Kilson argues that I support "the mindless hip-hop style irreverence toward African-American civil rights leadership," and that I consider it "some kind of *new freedom* for Black actors and entertainers to verbally dishonor Dr. King, Rosa Parks, and others." Further, he says I approach the "analytically bizarre" when in my op-ed I claim that "the barbershop . . . may be one of the last bastions of unregulated speech in black America," and that, at their worst, civil rights organizations are "antidemocratic institutions headed by gifted but authoritarian leaders."

Kilson goes on to say that my "outright falsehoods" are "analytically wrong and serve as anti-Black ammunition for conservative opponents of African-Americans' civil rights agenda." He says that millions of black folk find voice through their leaders in civil rights organizations. Further, open speech was the point of "Negro spirituals, gospel music, the 'dozens,' dinner table-talk, street talk, [and] meetings of all kinds of African-American organizations." Kilson concludes that I might do "well to revisit the folk essence of African-American institutions" before I again contemplate "an affront to Black people's honor."

What Kilson fails to grasp is that the hip hop community has become a dominant African American institution. Where young black Americans once turned primarily to the church—and to the civil rights leaders that the church produced—to articulate their hopes, frustrations, and daily tribulations, it is fast becoming men like Jay-Z and Nas, and women like Missy Elliot and Lauryn Hill, who best vocalize the struggle of growing up black and poor in this country.

Nevertheless, Kilson captures what many black folks believe about hip hop, and those scholars associated with its defense. Many agree with Kilson that "there's *nothing whatever that's seriously radical or progressive about hip hop ideas and values.*" Many support Kilson's view that hip hop is little more "than an updated face on the old-hat, crude, anti-humanistic values of hedonism and materialism."

Hip hop's critics make a valid point that the genre is full of problematic expressions. It reeks of materialism; it feeds on stereotypes and offensive language; it spoils with retrogressive views; it is rife with hedonism; and it surely doesn't always side with humanistic values. But the arguments of many of hip hop's critics demand little engagement with hip hop. Their views don't require much beyond attending to surface symptoms of a culture that offers far more depth and color when it's taken seriously and criticized thoughtfully. It is odd that so many gifted intellectuals should so resolutely stick to superfluous observation. Such critics seem afraid of the intellectual credibility or complex truths they might find were they to surrender their sideline seat and take an analytical plunge into the culture on which they comment.

It would be outlandish for critics to comment on, say, metaphysical poetry without interacting critically with its most inspired poets. At least *read* Donne. And if one were to make hay over the virtues or deficits of nineteenth-century British poetry or twentieth-century Irish poetry, then one should encounter the full range of Tennyson's or Yeats's work before jumping, or slouching, to conclusions. I'm afraid that many critics, including Kilson, haven't done their homework. That's characteristic of the sniping posture of many defensive elders who haven't put their gifts to good use in the guise of cultural critic. Like Kilson, many critics end up wearing their feelings on their peeves.

The dead giveaway is that many critics like Kilson take on articles—op-eds to be exact—and not the books of the scholars I noted above. It is intellectually lazy of Kilson in particular to take such a tack, since he's renowned for his erudition. What better way to make a straw argument than by parsing words in a less-than-thousand-word article while refusing to engage a text that actually takes on these issues in far more sophisticated and demanding fashion—perhaps too demanding for one out to make book on thin premises. The major points in my *New York Times* op-ed on the brouhaha over *Barbershop*, stirred largely by civil rights leaders, were that films are not scholarly monographs; that folk have the right to express themselves, and if we don't like it, we can criticize them or make our own films; that one film can't possibly represent the entire black experience; that recent scholarship focused on mass movements in the civil rights era veered toward group dynamics being just as important as charismatic leadership; that civil rights organizations *at their worst* shut down free speech; that *at its best* an informal community gathering place like a barbershop offers politically incorrect black speech as a bonus with sheared hair; and that art is supposed to get in our faces and not simply soothe or reassure us.

What Kilson failed to mention is that I've written a book on rapper Tupac Shakur and one on Dr. King. But Kilson couldn't acknowledge that since it would ruin his argument, much as the critics of hip hop don't want to spoil their biases through concrete engagements with the culture they despise. I don't despise civil rights; I take it so seriously that I engage it at fair length, concluding that, despite his faults, King is the greatest American produced on our native soil. The goals and ideals of the civil rights movement are so important to me that I work feverishly to bring those concepts to bear on the debates happening in this country today. Rather than relegate our past leaders to the celebratory pages of history, I want to engage them and see what their teachings and their examples can tell us about our current condition. It is not meant as blasphemy to consult Dr. King when discussing Tupac; rather, it is an admission that King's message still resonates and has consequence though times are different and the culture has evolved. The study of hip hop is not a repudiation of the civil rights movement. It is an effort to bridge the gap between then and now, and to offer the insight of past icons to the younger generation while engaging young folks' criticisms of their elders.

Hip hop needs to be called out for its lesser qualities, for its abysmal failures. But hip hop's critics ignore how some of the sharpest criticism comes from within hip hop's borders. The first line of Jay-Z's inspiring comeback album, *Kingdom Come*, laments the sorry state of current hip hop: "The game's f***** up / Niggas beats is banging / Nigga ya hooks did it / Ya lyrics didn't / Ya gangsta look did it." And Nas's stirring *Hip Hop Is Dead* is an album-length autopsy of hip hop's rapper mortis: "Everybody sound the same, commercialize the game / Reminiscin' when it wasn't all business / They forgot where it started / So we all gather here for the dearly departed." The difference between such criticisms, and those made by critics who fail to engage hip hop as a complex and immensely varied art form, is the balance and the historical memory at work in the best musical and literary commentary on the culture. Outside of the criticism offered on hip hop albums, rigorous engagement and sustained critique occur in the books that Kilson and other critics must wrestle with beyond tackling newspaper articles.

Kilson's shameless anti-intellectualism on this score is shared by other writers like Hugh Pearson, a Brown University graduate who is appalled by the fact that Ivy League schools like Harvard and Penn would dare offer hip hop courses. Writing in *Newsday*, Pearson condemns Harvard's Du Bois Institute for housing a hip hop archive because its scholars deem the art form and culture on which it rests to be worthy of study. Pearson's condescension is barely concealed; he rails at rappers with "a tendency to compose ungrammatical lyrics flowing from the ungrammatical speech patterns that are standard for too many African-Americans." Unlike earlier funk musicians, who "in those days no one considered . . . worthy of 'study' at a serious university," Pearson is galled that the Ivy League "will now treat hip hop as respectable."

Pearson has no sense of irony when he pinches a phrase from a man of manifest mediocrity, George W. Bush, who in accepting the Republican nomination for the presidency at its 2000 convention spoke of the "soft bigotry of low expectations." It was an unintended autobiography in précis for the future president. Pearson samples the line to suggest that's what studying hip hop in the academy amounts to. He argues that the study of hip hop, instead of "[raising] cultural standards . . . prefers to make chicken salad out of chicken necks."

In putting down the study of hip hop, and African American studies as well, Pearson contends that it's simply unworthy of serious examination. But I maintain that we should be willing to take a scholarly look at hip hop for no other reason than it has grabbed global attention and sparked emulation in countless different countries and among varied ethnicities. For example, when I was in Brazil to speak recently, I visited the Black Six, a hip hop club in Rio. I might as well have been in Harlem or Philadelphia, since the dance, dress, drinks, and music were all the same. The way cultural expression traverses international boundaries and is adopted in languages and accents indigenous to each region is itself a cause of intellectual curiosity.

It is telling that Pearson resists the impulse of true scholars and intellectuals to probe the cultural contexts and social meanings of art forms that demand the world's attention in the way hip hop has over the past quarter century. Pearson appears to be ashamed of hip hop, a feeling he shares with many blacks and others who decry its sordid images as the refuse of the culture that should be taken away with the garbage. Pearson's shame prevents him from acknowledging just how interesting and insightful the study of rap has proved around the world. His demand that world-class universities ignore hip hop is an odd cry for remedial provincialism: a return to a climate of academic curiosity where only a narrow range of subjects could be legitimately pursued.

This brief discussion should show just why the study of hip hop is so critical. By taking the time to explain a fertile culture of expression, students of hip hop place at our disposal some of the most intriguing investigations of a powerful art form. Unlike McWhorter, intellectuals who study hip hop don't shy away from probing the complex varieties of black identity, even those that skirt close to stereotype, as they undress its mauling effects in stunted visions of black female identity. Unlike Kilson, the best "hip hop intellectuals" dig deep into hip hop's rich traditions of expression to generate a criticism equal to the art that inspires it. And unlike Pearson, such intellectuals have no shame in poring hard and long over hip hop; they assume its intellectual value without being unduly defensive about its critical status.

The global impact of hip hop is being studied by scholars like Deborah Wong at the University of California–Riverside, who covers Asian hip hop, and Marcyliena Morgan at Stanford University, who researches hip hop in Cuba and England. The methodologies of examining hip hop are borrowed from sociology, politics, religion, economics, urban studies, journalism, communications theory, American studies, transatlantic studies, black studies, history, musicology, comparative literature, English, linguistics, and other disciplines. Hip hop has long since proved that it is no cultural or intellectual fad. Its best artists and intellectuals are as capable of stepping back and critiquing its flows and flaws as the most astute observers and participants in any other genre of musical or critical endeavor. As the academic study of hip hop enters a new phase—as it matures and expands, as it deepens and opens up even broader avenues of investigation—its advocates must wrestle with the many-sided features of a dynamic culture that demands serious consideration.

Hip hop scholarship must strive to reflect the form it interrogates, offering the same features as the best hip hop: seductive rhythms, throbbing beats, intelligent lyrics, soulful samples, and a sense of joy that is never exhausted in one sitting. The book you hold in your hand is my attempt to wrestle with the creative cultural expressions of often degraded black youth that have garnered them international acclaim. It is also my effort to pursue several other ends: to probe the vexed gender relations and sexual politics that have made rap music a lightning rod for wags and pundits; to explore the commercial explosion of an art form that has made it vulnerable to contradiction and a victim of its own success; to examine the political elements that have been submerged in the most popular form of hip hop while creating a vibrant underground; and to intellectually engage with some of hip hop's most influential figures.

I also aim to match hip hop's verbal acrobatics and linguistic innovation with my knowledge of the culture in the form of the long interview, which I have sought to remake as the intellectual's version of hip hop lyrical invention. One gets a sense in interviews on hip hop of the improvisational flavor and rhetorical creativity that mark the genre at its best. *Know What I Mean?* is the first attempt to achieve such a goal between the covers of a book—in the style and format of a hip hop album. I hope to offer a rousing intellectual complement to an art form that has seized and colored the global imagination. This is my best argument for the study of hip hop culture, and for the intellectual examination and self-criticism that it provokes.

KNOW WHAT I MEAN?

And what I'm writin', is guaranteed to enlighten /
like Dr. Cornel West, Michael Eric Dyson.

—*KRS-ONE, "The Mind"*

TRACK 1.

"HOW REAL IS THIS?"

CREDITS

Guest Artist: *Meta DuEwa Jones*

Label: *University of Texas at Austin*

Studio Location: *Austin and Philadelphia*

Year Recorded: *2006*

Samples: *Michel Foucault * Immanuel Kant * G. F. W. Hegel * Tupac Shakur * Howard Thurman * Lauryn Hill * Max Weber * Toni Morrison * The Hebrew Bible (The Psalms) * W. E. B. Du Bois * V. Y. Mudimbe * Killah Priest*

Shout Outs: *Black Authenticity * Realism * Pimping * Class Conflict * Prison-Industrial Complex * Home-i-cide * Technology and Art * Hustle & Flow * Political Economy of Sex*

Head Nods: *2Pac * 50 Cent * Lil' Kim * Foxy Brown * Eve * Missy Elliott * Jay-Z * Master P * Killah Priest * Lauryn Hill*

"HOW REAL IS THIS?"

Prisons, iPods, Pimps, and the Search for Authentic Homes

Meta DuEwa Jones: You're a scholar, an ordained minister, a philosopher, and the author of numerous books exploring black expressive cultures, one of which focuses on Tupac Shakur. You're also an African American. Could you speak from that perspective about who is authorized to interpret and articulate hip hop's past, present, and future?

Michael Eric Dyson: There's been a pretty consistent historical framework for interpreting black cultures.

Black humanity and art have always been viewed, on the one hand, with suspicion and skepticism and, on the other hand, with paranoia and fear. It's true that many white folk have admired our culture and interpreted it through the lens of their experience. Many whites have loved and identified with black culture while maintaining intellectual distortions, avoidances, and obstructions. Some outside the race think that if they study the culture and learn from its artists and thinkers, they are qualified to interpret and analyze black culture. I don't disagree with that conclusion. Color can't be the basis for analyzing culture because some of the best insight on black folk has come from white brothers and sisters. Conversely, some of the most leaden and unimaginative interpretations of black life have come from black folk.

So I'm not saying that non–black folk can't understand and interpret black culture. But there *is* something to be said for the dynamics of power, where nonblacks have been afforded the privilege to interpret and—given the racial politics of the nation—to legitimate or decertify black vernacular and classical culture in ways that have been denied to black folk. So it's not simply a question of the mastery of a set of ideas associated with the interpretation or appraisal of black life and art. It's also about the power to shape a lens through which this culture is interpreted, and is seen as legitimate, or viable, or desirable, or real, by the dominant culture. That is at stake as well.

Jones: You use the word "legitimate." But the word that is always coming up in relationship to hip hop and its interpretation—aesthetically, politically, and culturally—is "authenticity." The question I asked before leads to the question about *who* can authentically interpret black culture. But I'm also interested in whether you see, in hip hop's future, shifts in who can authentically not only *represent* hip hop, but who can authentically *perform* it, *record* it, and *produce* it? Could you please talk a bit about hip hop and its relationship to authenticity in African American culture?

Dyson: There are multiple streams of authenticity flowing at the same time. What's interesting about hip hop, versus earlier forms of black oral and aesthetic expression, is that there's a big investment by hip hop artists in defining authenticity.

That is not to say that earlier artists weren't strongly invested in the stakes of authenticity. Bebop was an inspired response from the streets to forms of jazz that had been coopted by whites. The polyrhythmic structures of African American vernacular music rang out against diluted jazz music from white musicians who had taken over swing and jump music. Bebop, in large part, was a rebellion against the white appropriation of the music that implied an authentic politics of aesthetic expression. So there was a huge investment going on there.

But never before has the debate over authenticity

been as resonant as it is in hip hop culture. Hip hop's original makers and producers, African Americans and Latinos, were especially conscious of the authenticity debate from the beginning, perhaps because their culture was under assault by older members of black culture and society at large. I think because they were doubted and dismissed, hip hoppers were heavily invested in specifying what's real and what's not.

When black people come up with forms of cultural expression that are narrow and rigid—essentialist—they're often in response to the attempt to impose vicious, or racist, or stereotypical views of black life from outside our culture. Essentialism is often conjured by bigotry and attack. We've got to see things in that dynamic give-and-take, because there's a cleavage that's being created, a real dichotomy: having something imposed on a culture versus attempting to identify the legitimate outlines of that culture from within.

You definitely see that going on in hip hop. And its investment in the authenticity debates is even bigger because of the political context in which hip hop has developed—aesthetic put-downs, derision of its musical and cultural contributions, doubt about whether it is a permanent or passing form of music, accusations of adding pathological and nihilistic elements to the culture. All of this stuff guarantees that hip hop, more than any other form of African American cultural and musical expression, will obsess over who can produce it and record it.

These fights over authenticity take place along a couple of divides. There's the rift between underground hip hop and commercial rap. The underground claims to be an authentic expression of a kind of hip hop that has not been emptied of its moral or aesthetic meaning by commercial dictates. For example, it resists white music executives who would rather watch rappers feature a black female shaking her behind and bouncing her bosom or a black male "rolling on twenties with the top down," than hear them talking about resisting racial injustice and economic oppression. So that's one divide.

The other divide is between ghettocentric black culture and bourgeois Negro expression. There's a class division between those who are willing to "ride or die" for poor black people whose backs are against the wall—so that rap's pavement poetry vibrates with commitment to speaking for the voiceless—and those who are unapologetically elitist and "bourgie." Being elitist isn't simply a matter of having money and upward mobility. Some rappers themselves got a whole bunch of money.

But I'm referring to a certain kind of bourgeois mindset, a kind of elitist perspective, one that affects how you see aesthetic expression. Back in the nineteenth century, black people put forth the notion of uplift. It was about representing the authentic character of black people as noble and edifying and enlightened—versus the streets that expressed the "basest" element of African American culture. We see that debate playing itself out today in the tensions between bourgeois blacks who are shamed and chagrined by poor blacks, and other blacks who are either rooted in or moved by the exigencies, the limits, the concerns, and the preoccupations of the black poor.

And finally, a generational divide looms large in black life. When it comes to culture and the like, a lot of older black folk simply baptize their biases and make them the basis of what is authentic about black life, particularly when it comes to culture. The time period they grew up in becomes the golden age, and the music they grew up with during that golden age becomes the ideal expression of the black aesthetic. Everything else is judged against that norm, and is usually found wanting. What's funny is that the music of their youth was often negatively judged by *their* elders. But that doesn't seem to stop each generation from generating its own standards, tastes, preferences, and dislikes—which is fine by me, except I don't think you can claim exclusive rights to the authentic or the moral on that basis alone. You've got to make arguments based on more than age and epoch.

A lot of older folk—and some younger ones too—look at hip hop and conclude that young artists are simply newfangled jiggaboos who are repackaging stereotypical representations of black popular culture. Their art is written off as little more than the pathology of insidious white supremacist ideas wrapped in black skin. Of course, the artists who are obsessed with the holy trinity of contemporary rap—broads, booze, and bling—make it that much harder on the rest of the hip hop world. But in the minds of their elders, they're not authentic at all; they're just reflections of the negative beliefs about black folk that the dominant culture has dropped on us. Ultimately, all of these debates—underground versus commercial, bourgeois versus poor, and old versus young—are really debates about what's best seen as black, and what's seen as the best of our blackness, the most authentic form of black identity.

Jones: You have used the terms "Afristocracy" and "Ghettocracy" to talk about the class divide. Could you say a little about how class markers function in the context of hip hop, in terms of perception and reality?

Dyson: Actual class relations notwithstanding, the lure of the ghetto resides in its symbolic representation of the socially and economically vulnerable. Within hip hop, there is a certain narrative protocol that means you stop by the ghetto just to pay your respects. This evokes another politics of authenticity, one that says, "Aha, these people are really faking, because they're bourgeois. They're Negroes from the suburbs of New York, or Long Island. They went to school; they're not really from the hood."

As if somebody who is middle class can't imagine what it means to have lethal social limits imposed on you. Such a limiting view of authenticity suggests that artists can't inherit stories of the ghetto from others who have been there. This view of authenticity is as limited as the ghettocentric one, since it seems to argue that unless you've lived it, you can't write or sing it.

But that's the magic of artists: they can inhabit spaces and ideas and worldviews they have never actually touched or tasted. The purpose of an artist is not necessarily to live the experience to which he or she refers, even though the gospel refrain, "I want to live the life I sing about in my song," means something far different than the arbiters of authenticity are aiming at. In the gospel world, it has to do with behaving in a way that does not contradict the ideals you stand for and the ones you sing about. An artistic creation has integrity because your life does. It's not necessarily the same in pop music.

Does anyone challenge Madonna? I mean, she's been through nine different phases. First she was a virgin, then she was a material girl, then she was a postreligious vagabond, then a universal, omnisexual whore. Now she's a devout student of kabbalah. All along, she's been making hits, selling records. Does anyone take Frank Sinatra's origins to task? You know, he derived huge symbolic capital from an alleged connection, shadowy as it was, to the mob. Whether it was literally true or not is almost irrelevant because the power of his symbolic attachment forged a material connection to the Mafia in the minds of many.

So I think that when it comes to hip hop, things function in the same way. The metaphysical root of hip hop is connected to the ghetto whether or not many of its artists grew up there. It's almost irrelevant to me whether or not you grew up there. It's more important to know if you're able to scrutinize the possibilities, the positions, the moods, the dispositions, the interests, the sentiments, and the morality that the environment breeds. If you're able to tap into those things and understand what they might mean—if you're able to imagine in your art the story and myth that should be told—that's just as fine as being there.

In a way, the arguments over authenticity in hip hop are signs of its strength in selling a story, in marketing itself as a specific kind of art with a narrative through line. The great irony is that the critics of hip hop have been uncritical in buying the story that hip hop has been telling about itself, with little critical distance from the mythology. So the self-description of hip hop has taken over any "objective" examination of the form. The hip hop notion that if you ain't poor and black you ain't authentic may have been generated by folk outside of the ghetto. A lot of people in the ghetto are trying to get the hell up out of there. They don't want to romanticize it. So it's not the ghetto that's being romanticized—its physical geography—so much as the intellectual attachment and intimacy that it breeds, a bond established among those who suffer and struggle together who long for an exit from its horrible limits.

So in that sense, the ghetto functions as an intellectual organizing principle of expression, and the logic of the ghetto—or at least the logic of legitimating the ghetto in rap discourse—depends on understanding the complex and contradictory interests of the people who live there. A lot of people want to defend the demonized individuals who emerge from the ghetto just as much as they want to leave it behind. But I think that kind of thing is often overlooked in many discussions of hip hop because the intellectual merit of the hip hop artist is not on par with artists of other fields. Nobody thinks that Arnold Schwarzenegger or Bruce Willis or Sylvester Stallone literally engages in the behavior they act on screen.

Now, true enough, they are not part of a culture that brags about keeping things real, as is the case with some hip hoppers who can't distinguish between what they're doing on records and what they're doing in their crib. I acknowledge, and make allowances for, that difference. But at the same time, the brilliant intellectual energy and imagination that fuel hip hop at its best, which can generate a mythology of authenticity rooted in the ghetto, is often ignored. After all, realism in any genre is hard work.

For instance, realism in film is not made by taking a camera and training it on a block for a week and calling it a film. Realism depends on mythopoetics. Realism depends on artifice and fiction to create its narrative thrust. And hip hoppers have understood that from the very beginning. They've winked with one eye and played the politics of authenticity even as they pulled away from it and called it into question. Of course some of them take it quite literally—there are debates about whether certain artists are as big a hustler as they claim. But even Malcolm X was accused of exaggerating his hustler's résumé to emphasize the moral distance he had to cover to become a devout spiritual man. It works the same way in hip hop.

But ultimately, as Tupac understood and as cultural theorist Michel Foucault argued, one's very life can be a work of art. Hence authenticity didn't consist so much in relating one's work to oneself, but in relating one's life to a creative activity. Should an authentic model of reality inform the art, or vice versa? Can life be informed by the protocols and machinations of art? Can art be a source of moral and ethical energy that should be transmitted to others who engage in serious self-reflection? Why can't that be the case? I think seeing things this way is part of the ingenuity of hip hop.

And what do great artists do? They see and they say. They don't have to live it, but they can make you believe they've lived it. It's the same with the politics of authenticity. Within hip hop the elevation of the ghetto is often a metaphysical complaint against society's failure to recognize the humanity of those who come from the ghetto. And by the same token, hip hop artists are rarely given credit for the kind of intellectual ingenuity it takes to create narratives that spark debates about whether what they say is true or not. That's a great deal of the ingenuity of the art form itself. Also, I think very few people are willing to acknowledge the genius of our black children.

Jones: Much is made of someone like 50 Cent's authenticity story in terms of the number of times he's been shot and whether or not he's had affiliations with the prison-industrial complex. Do you see this portraying prison as a home or as a holding cell, as something that is being critiqued in hip hop?

Dyson: Young black men have embraced—and to an extent transformed—certain elements of the prison-industrial complex: the sagging pants, the baggy shirts, the laceless shoes, and the like. Of course, part of the fascination with prison is a reflection of the sad existential truths of young black male life; as the philosopher Immanuel Kant might say, a necessity is turned into a virtue. I say necessity because the near ubiquitous presence of prison in the social landscape of black male life means that it increasingly seems natural for black males to go to jail—or even to want to go to jail, as a place they have allegiance to, a space where they shape a large part of their identity. In that case, we'll have to come up with the category of the "tragic natural," since to see your life as a black male best realized behind bars, because the society throws you few other options, means that you're already in a kind of psychological and spiritual prison.

Ain't nothing natural about being locked up like an animal—locked away from your family and friends. That's why there's such a big emphasis in young black male life on "my niggas," or those cats you learn to love like family because you've all been thrown by social circumstance and personal choice into a ghetto, a project, a slum, a gang, a crew, a cell block, a tribe, or some other social order. So to link black machismo, authenticity, and incarceration is undeniably a horrible thing, but it's often one of the few choices that a lot of young black males have. To believe that your manhood is best tested and developed in prison is nothing short of bizarre and tragic. And hip hop has both challenged this and reinforced it at the same time. It has both gasped at the horror of the "pen" and glamorized it all the same. And even if cats ain't spent time in prison themselves, they've got a great deal of vicarious identification with those who have.

We see this in some of Tupac's early music, talking about going there, about being locked up. He knows, or believes he does, that he's going to end up there. "Much love to my brothers in the pen / See ya when I free ya if not when they shove me in." So it's almost the inevitable . . .

Jones: Or "I'll call you when I get out."

Dyson: Exactly. So you're either on your way to prison, or on your way from prison. Or you're in prison. And yeah, that's endlessly and unavoidably metaphoric, especially in regard to black masculinity and the black male body, which is seen by some as being imprisoned by the broader culture. The black body is constantly being assaulted by the withering force of injustice that seeks to warehouse black men in the burgeoning prison-industrial complex. The sense of inevitability black men experience about going to prison didn't fall from the sky; it's not simply the idealization of prison as a point of departure, intellectually, for black men. It's not hard to imagine where a lot of black men get that idea from. A lot of us end up there! And before we go there a lot of us are told that's where we're going to end up. So it doesn't take much imagination to conjure the prison as an alternative home.

In that light, it's not hard to understand why so many young black male artists create myths and stories about prison, since many of them are told from day one that it's their ultimate, inevitable, logical, deserved domicile. This is what happens when we see certain cultures, and subcultures, through the lens of pathology. The scholar V. Y. Mudimbe talks about the pathologization of the urban. Well, part of the pathologization of the urban is the demonization of the young black male, and increasingly the young black female. For those who buy into such notions of pathology, the only suitable resolution to the intrinsic pathology of young black life is the curative space of the penitentiary. You must do penitence in the Quaker sense, and that's where the term originally derived its meaning. One must seek redemption by going into a pen and reconstructing, reshaping, refabricating one's essential identity. One must remake his sense of a moral home. If your home resides now in criminalized ambitions, it must be remade to reside in uplifting moral intent.

The notion of prison as home makes it a place of both discipline and rest, as well as, ironically enough, nurture and hospitality. Finding hospitable spaces within the prison-industrial complex is an act of collusion between the warped desires of young black men, who've been led to embrace prison's necessity, and the state, which seeks to impose a sense of familiarity, of home-fulness, on young black men and women. And if we just play with the words, is there any wonder that so many young black men kill each other, commit homicide—home-i-cide? Even domicide—a murder of their sense of identification, their home-fulness and dwelling with their brothers, since one of the most effective tools of social control under white supremacy is the psychological destruction of the image of the black male in the mind of another black male.

In light of this, we have to deal with the political circumstances that feed the artistic and social imagination of black men and fuel a racist, repressive state. Of course, this isn't the first time the collective imagination of black men has been filled with prison narratives and images. For instance, during the 1960s civil rights movement, imprisonment stories had a religious bent. Prison was a place to extend protest, or to fashion stories that transcended the iron bars folk had to endure. It was hardly romanticized as a place to craft black manhood, except to suggest that black men who were willing to pay the price of unjust imprisonment were real heroes.

Martin Luther King Jr. went to prison; some of the best prophets in the culture went to prison. But it reminds me of what the great prophetic mystic Howard Thurman said, that those who rise above the moral level of society and those who fall beneath it face the same consequence. Jesus, after all, is on a cross between two thieves. So those who challenge the moral authority of the state, and those who fall beneath its laws and strictures, are all at once summoned to receive the same penalty. Martin Luther King Jr. was shot and killed. Malcolm X was shot and killed. Medgar Evers was shot and killed. All of them were good, even great men who challenged malevolent forces, both in the larger society and, at least in Malcolm's case, from within his own group.

We cannot help but conclude that prison has become a warehouse for young black men who are falling beneath the law, as well as for those who challenge it, even if mostly in a metaphorical way. Their stinging words are imprisoned. Their revolutionary thoughts are interned. Their rhetoric is locked away. But this doesn't just happen outside the culture; there are even moves to contain the rhetoric of hip hop within black life. That's why hip hop culture is subject to punitive measures doled out by the defenders of a narrow black moral discourse. There are many black forces that seek to imprison the "outlaw" rhetoric of young folk viewed as subversive agents of a destructive black ethical identity.

So to me, for all parties concerned, prison is infinitely metaphorical. It works in a number of ways. But at the end of the day, to just be real fundamental, Amnesty International came and did a report about America that said the same infraction young (white) Jill and Johnny are slapped on the back of the hand for, young (black) Shaniqua and Shaquille are warehoused in juvenile detention centers, where they practice for their ultimate home—the big house, the stone hotel, the prison-industrial complex.

So the conspiracy of the state, as well as the forces in the culture that demonize and arrest the development of young black men and women through narratives of shame and displeasure, ultimately derive from the same limiting and punitive place. Under these circumstances, there is little merit to the notion that prison can provide a space of intellectual engagement and liberation. Tupac claimed that, contrary to those who said prison was a place of fruitful artistic reflection, he was stymied by it. He didn't write from jail like the Apostle Paul did. He didn't write from jail like Benjamin Chavis did. He didn't write from jail like many other cats, because they went with a different moral purpose, which shows it wasn't the prison . . .

Jones: Even from a cell like King did . . .

Dyson: Right. Because he went there for a different pur-pose. The point is that the prison became a way station to a larger moral and political social purpose. It wasn't the be-all and end-all. For younger cultures and dissident cultures, the prison has been romanticized as the source of thought. But it's not; rather, it is the backdrop for a certain moral register. King's purpose became more prominent when he was unfairly housed in a prison.

The tragedy is that the unfair imprisonment of black men and women cannot be distinguished from the gen-eral plight of young blacks because moral stories that criminalize young people obscure the truth that a lot of them are going there for no good reason. Although the disparity in prison sentencing for those who use crack and those who use blow is awful, a lot of black folk obsess over the crime of drug abuse and not the crime of unjust sentencing. I'm not saying they shouldn't be concerned about the former, but they should spend a lot more time on the latter. Black folks' moralizing often blots out the truth that some folk will predictably make mistakes in a political economy where poverty is nearly guaranteed if they can't get educated.

Because education is related to the economic position you have in the society, there's a vicious, circular charac-ter to the homelessness that black people face in the state and in domestic spaces and subsequently, when they are thrust into the external regions of the prison. The prison performs the functions of home for so many people. At least they have "three hots and a cot": three meals a day, plus a place to lay their heads. Those are luxuries that some of them can't get in the free world—where they're free to starve and free to be homeless in some cases.

Jones: How does the link between black machismo, authenticity, and incarceration that you discussed resonate with the difficult and sometimes demeaning sexual and gender politics of hip hop in the realms of rhetoric, performance, and visual culture?

Dyson: Well, I'll restate the obvious for purposes of underscoring our solidarity with those who find deeply misogynistic lyrics offensive. You resonate with that, I resonate with that. When it comes to the performance of black masculinity in hip hop culture or the creative spaces that are available for females, you're dealing with something just as problematic as misogynist lyrics. There just isn't much room for independent women in rap music and hip hop culture.

When you survey the landscape, here's what you get: the extension of the crotch politics of black machismo; the subordination of female desire to male desire; the recolonizing of the black female body by the imperialistic gaze of the black male. Black men want to dominate women according to their own sexual desire. They issue sexual edicts about the bodies of the women who come within their circle of influence. The price of admission in that culture is a surrender of sexual autonomy by the women in order to please the desires of men. All of those have nothing to do with lyrics.

Within the broader political economy of hip hop culture, it's doubtful that women can consistently negotiate the unfair demands and ridiculous rules of becoming recording producers or executives. So for me, there's not a severe disconnect between misogyny on records and the sexism and the patriarchy—or the term I've coined, "femiphobia," the sheer fear of women—in the rest of hip hop.

But then again, the limited success that women have enjoyed in hip hop—as lawyers, managers, and of course some record executives—should challenge the narrow roles imagined for women by some of its lyricists and rhetoricians. This stuff didn't start with hip hop; the reality is that patriarchy and sexism and misogyny are tried-and-true American traditions from which hip hop derives its understanding of how men and women should behave, and what roles they should play. But these ancient forms of sexism and patriarchy and misogyny and femiphobia that shape the personal and business relationships between men and women in hip hop culture are rarely brought into view when the focus is on young black folk.

In other words, it ain't hip hop that's teaching the broader culture how to dog a woman; it's the broader culture's ways and rules that are keyed in by hip hop lyricists. That means that women have a hard time on the creative side with the lyrics that you spoke about, and in the political dimensions of gender as well.

In terms of the performance of gender by females, some female lyricists are trying to appropriate the dominant machismo of the culture and flip it, so that the vagina becomes the second womb, the source of a rebirthing of black female identity as a mirror image of what the men are doing. If the penis is the magic stick, then the vagina is the organ that takes the magic stick—a one-up(wo)manship, so to speak. You can see this in Lil' Kim, Foxy Brown, and in some of the more explicit sexual raps that imagine black women as reverse lotharios, so to speak: women who are able to "mack" their game, and express their sexual autonomy by seducing and controlling the black man. So what they're seeking to do is flip the script and change the politics by simply changing the subject of domination and the object of control.

I think Eve and Missy Elliot are seeking to express a sense of female identity that is independent of black masculinity. Because when you look at certain moments in their careers—you look at the rap about abuse that Eve creates, or you look at the fact that Missy Elliot produces records by other female artists who pleasure themselves—you see interesting elements of female identity cropping up, regardless of their references to black phalluses or other representations of black masculine sexuality. So, at that level, they play both ends against the middle, so to speak. They can both dip into and sample the culture of black masculine sexuality, but they're also interested in probing this other side that has nothing to do with that black masculinity, and they're seeking the politics . . .

Jones: Of sexual autonomy, within a sexual economy.

Dyson: Right, within the political economy of sex. It's about self-pleasuring versus depending on a man to please oneself. That challenges the political economy of patriarchy, because a big part of patriarchy's calling card is intimidation through insemination. Of course, patriarchy can dominate even in the absence of its power to inseminate. Even an impotent phallus is powerful because its owner can take out its resentment on vulnerable bodies. More broadly, I think the performance of black female identity as a response to black male sexuality can be problematic.

But certain protests against the exploitative uses of black female sexuality are helpful. Think about Lauryn Hill's point in "(Doo Wop) That Thing," when she says, "It's been three weeks since you've been looking for your friend / The one you let hit it and never called you again." The guy didn't call you back after he had sex with you because you got played. And you got played because you became his sexual object and toy. She says, "Plus when you give it up so easy you ain't even foolin' him / If you did it then, then you'd probably f— again." There's some feminist resistance to women being subordinated to black sexual desire in the lyrics of some female MCs.

But it's rare that females in hip hop are able to express an alternative worldview where their ideas, interests, and agendas are taken seriously.

Jones: When we talk about the gender politics of hip hop, we can't get away from its relationship to the politics of film. The most recent, and infamous, example is the film *Hustle & Flow*. Some critics contended that although this is a pimp story, the pimp has a heart of gold, and thus the film's importance isn't really about him being in a position to exploit women. Could you talk a bit about the film in terms of its vision of hip hop and gender, and also in terms of its relationship to technology? Because the pimp character is also an aspiring rapper— there's a kind of politics of ascendancy, a revamped Horatio Alger story of going from rags to riches. But he's also making a demo tape in an era in which there are CDs, and now MP3s.

Dyson: I think the film is quite provocative and conceptually fertile. *Hustle & Flow* is to pimpdom what Clint Eastwood's *Unforgiven* is to the Western: a visual deconstruction and cinematic undoing of the very mythology on which the pimp rests. The symbolism of the pimp in black American culture is tied up with notions of upward mobility, especially when the pimp is viewed as providing an escape hatch for the economically degraded working-class man. Of course that upward mobility comes at the expense of the women beneath the pimp—sometimes literally—who supply the erotic labor on which his rise depends.

In brutally direct fashion, the pimp seizes control of the female's reproductive organs to make money and generate status for himself. Pimping, in certain ways, both simulates and replicates chattel slavery, or the owning of bodies for the purposes of generating wealth. Pimping is the plantation in motion. The pimp is at once master and overseer, wielding control over the subordinate body of the ho. Pimping also brings to mind Hegel's master-slave dialectic—where the lines of domination and submission are blurred by the increasing independence of the slave and the growing dependence of the master on the slave—except it's written into a specific kind of sexual and social relationship between men and women.

Hustle & Flow demythologizes the pimp narrative and mythology, 'cause the pimp is poorer than his hoes! So the film twists the literal dependence of the pimp on his hoes (after all, the pimp depends on the economic earning power of his stable of women) to a spiritual and moral dependence. It's like he's a pimp who's got his game on layaway, and his hoes are going to get him out of debt. Or it's like he's a pimp with his game in a pawn shop, and his hoes are going to get him out of hock. Furthermore, this is a po' broke pimp with a bootleg car, with a "hooptie." One of the most powerful and potent phallic symbols— in pimping and in other masculine domains—is the car. This pimp got a broke-down ride! He ain't got no air conditioning. And not only that, he depends on the intellectual energies of his hoes, and he listens to them.

I don't want to make this a feminist tale, because it still takes place within the context of a pimp-ho relationship. But that being said, it's remarkable to what degree DJay, the film's pimp, relies on the intellectual insights of his hoes—whether it's his baby's mama, Shug, who is providing the hook for his raps and a lava lamp for inspiration, or the white ho, Nola, who always wanted to be more than a mere ho, who eventually takes over DJay's rap business while he's in jail. His other ho, Lexus, is an exotic dancer who is repulsed by DJay's inability to stand up and be vicious and aggressive like pimps are supposed to be. Ironically, it's her gesture of aggression toward DJay that compels him into a stereotypical posture of the pimp—beating his woman—conjuring in him repressed memories of the fantasy of dominance that should drive any pimp.

On the one hand, it can be argued that this is the most vicious politics of misogyny, because it is a ventriloquist act: it articulates black male desire through the voice of a woman. On the other hand, if social theorist Michel Foucault is right, and power is not centralized but breaks out everywhere, then the conflict between DJay and Lexus is a debate between Foucault and sociologist Max Weber on the celluloid screen. DJay is Foucault, and Lexus is Weber, because in her mind power resides in specific spaces and places in a hierarchy, with DJay on top and the hoes functioning beneath him at his behest. But if DJay is more like Foucault, then power is decentered and metastasizes across social relations. Power is shared between people who are relatively (though not equally) dominated by a culture in which they're seeking some sense of autonomy and agency. Whether or not we like the moral ambition or the ethical outcome, the bottom line is that even the hoes exercise agency.

There are still victims and women still don't come out on top, so to speak. But within the context of the film there are multiple sources of agency for the characters. There are ways in which women are giving and surrendering, but also taking back and reclaiming power. Yevette, the wife of Key, who is DJay's deejay and producer, has a negative view of DJay and his hoes because of her fundamentalist religious beliefs, but she gradually starts to understand and appreciate women who have to live in explicit ho-dom. The film doesn't probe this, but there's always the question of pitting women who work in the sex industry against homemakers and wives, and placing them in a similar situation of exploitation in relation to their husbands/pimps. After all, the work that women do within the political economy of a patriarchal household may not make them all that different from those who are forced into sex industries outside the home. All in all, it is a brilliant film to play off of, and to illumine the treacherous politics and the tortured consciences of those who participate in the oldest profession.

Now, in terms of technology, it is very interesting that in the midst of the primal forces of pimping, there's also an argument for the crudest, most basic dimensions of technology, and for the politics of the underground. Ironically, even though the underground is known for its progressive politics, in *Hustle & Flow* its ethical messages and warnings are carried in the throat of a pimp. It's even more interesting to note that the situation of the pimp's music production—Djay laboring in his home with his fellow workers and his hoes—is an argument for an old-school approach to recording. This is about the culture of the tape, this is about recalling the myth of hip hop origins. The iconography of the tape in an era of digital technology is like the ghetto version of Walter Benjamin's "The Work of Art in the Age of Mechanical Reproduction." It's about recording technology in the hands of those who control its content and reproduction.

And what's important here to DJay is the content of the tape. But the means by which the content is produced, the technological form in which the content is disseminated, has everything to do with respect for the production and source of hip hop culture. It's an ode to the "real" cats who were grinding on the block making tapes at the moment of his origin and emergence as a hip hopper.

Jones: You mean the moment . . .

Dyson: The moment DJay becomes a rapper, the moment he becomes an artist, is linked to his own understanding of what hip hop was about when Skinny Black, his idol, a local homeboy who made good as a rapper, was "blowing up." Making the tape is a way for DJay to call Skinny Black back to his origins. And the dialogue in the film supports that notion, especially the encounter in the bar between DJay and Skinny Black, when DJay has his finished product, his tape, in hand, ready to deliver it to Skinny Black personally, hoping that his remembrance of how he got started will kick in and make him respect DJay's efforts.

The ultimate symbol of his investment in his work—in the studio and by implication in his vocation as a pimp—comes when Skinny Black takes DJay's tape and asks him, "You stand by your product?" DJay replies, "Is a pig's pussy pork?" DJay also brings out Skinny Black's first tape as a reminder of his salad days, of hustling up the food chain to become a star, again hoping that it will evoke good memories of being on his grind and thus identifying with DJay's work ethic, as he gets his "hustle on." So DJay produces Skinny Black's first tape, but there's also a kind of poetic truth and license operating here. DJay has labored so hard to produce his own work that the lines are blurred between producing his own tape in the studio and producing Skinny Black's tape on the spot. DJay is suggesting that Skinny Black is a model and a metaphor for the production of his own tape. And since DJay has been a kind of apprentice, he produces the tape—the same means by which Skinny Black got started on his path to fame, hoping the same magic will rub off on him.

Producing a tape in the age of the CD is also about the quixotic politics of nostalgia linked to the authentic. This is about what's real. This is about how our culture has literally produced itself. Despite newfangled technologies and forms like the CD and MP3, what this is about—this production of a tape—is a man and his voice and his desire, and the people who conspire with him to create art that makes a difference to the soul. So I think part of that iconography of the tape is to contest the distancing and destabilizing and deracinating forces of technology, and to lift up the mom-and-pop store, the home production, the ability of the everyday person to invest his or her spirit in the production of a meaningful life.

All of that is being conjured at the same time. It strikes me, too, that the politics of artistic reproduction in *Hustle & Flow* explicitly feature women's minds and hands. Singing a hook, buying a lamp, and running a business spotlight female desire, work, and worth, sometimes ironically, at every level of the game. In the end, the tape helps keep its participants, and by extension Skinny Black, from a dangerous amnesia, a certain loss of community and identity that success can't protect against. So by producing his own tape and Skinny's tape, DJay calls Skinny down from the mountain of illusory success betokened in the CD to the valley of the tape, if I can borrow biblical language where Jesus told Peter that he couldn't stay on the mountain of Transfiguration, a space of joy and ecstasy and comfort, but that he had to return to the valley of suffering and grief and struggle where the masses lived. And the tape, the valley, is where DJay resides.

Jones: And the tape is home. In the film he says to Skinny Black, "I'm going back home."

Dyson: Absolutely.

Jones: I read an interview in which Toni Morrison said that there is no place African Americans can look back in history and find home. What is the home for hip hop in the future in an era when there are artists who are attempting to produce their work solely through Web production and Web circulation, as opposed to going the CD route or just selling them through downloading from iTunes. Could you talk a bit about the future home for hip hop in technological but also in metaphorical terms?

Dyson: I think technology imposes brutal confines and blunt restrictions on black life; conversely, in some ways technology opens up possibilities of self-expression or collective expression that are infinitely interesting. If technology is seen as playing a constructive role in furthering the concept and content of black domestic spaces, then in one sense that's consonant with the ever expanding, yet never quite existing context of home for black people. We found a place to stay and remained there. Or we were forced to find home in so many places that other people wouldn't ever be at home with. We were forced to "sing the Lord's songs in a strange land," as Psalm 137 famously says.

Remember, the children of Israel were in exile "by the rivers of Babylon," where the nation's members "wept when we remembered Zion," their home. Well, we were constantly faced with Babylon, with exile and homelessness. Babylon looms large in the metaphoric and symbolic universe of black speech. So that means, then, that black folk have constantly been preoccupied with a sense of home, and a sense of homelessness. That dialectic tension, that dichotomous existence—home and not home—was more than two different poles; it was also about the fusion of home and homelessness. Because even when we were home, we weren't home.

And then out on the road where other people couldn't even find a home, we managed to find places and spaces of intimacy, which, at least provisionally, accommodated our being, our deepest thoughts and emotions. So home was a process, not necessarily a place. Home was a verb for us, not necessarily a noun. It was a continual process of evolution, of claiming spaces and territories that were foreign, and domesticating and subordinating them in any way possible to our particular demands and needs.

In that sense, technology that seems deracinated— Web based as opposed to even a CD or involves us downloading songs onto our iPods—may be symbolic of the evolving, fluid process of home within African American culture. Historically, for many black folk, home was an ideal, an aspiration. Often out of cruel necessity, it was about a determination to have a certain state of mind, an approach, as opposed to a landing at a fixed space. There has been for us as a people a perennial frustration of the black quest for a suitable space to call our own. Therefore, calling something our own meant not simply ownership in the traditional sense but partnerships, symbiotic relationships with other people to own something. It meant trying to figure out the best way to lay claim to a particular process and imprint it with our identity, even if we didn't originate it.

You know, we didn't originate a lot of this technology, but we forced it into broader use. Look at the beeper, the pager, the cell phone—most of this technology was run through our communities first, or at least we made it viable, sexy, cool. Look at how that's been mythologized in

Master P's underground ghetto films, like "I Got the Hook Up." Interestingly enough, even stuff that gets universal recognition and distribution is sometimes first tried out in the hood. The ghetto becomes a global vetting space for the successful dissemination of products from the American marketplace. In that light, the term "black market" takes on a new meaning.

But look at another dimension of what black folk do with technology. I'm not saying we invented the mash-up—where the technology allows a gifted DJ to take existing music and vocals, reconfigure them, remix them, and then add music and vocals from another source, all the while keeping it in tune, at least ideally. You see this in DJ Danger Mouse's infamous underground classic mash-up *The Grey Album*, a fusion of Jay-Z's vocals from *The Black Album* and music from the Beatles' *The White Album*. It's clearly a nod to the strong improvisational elements of black culture. So our imprint on technology is much broader than simply what is vetted in ghettos.

It's also about the way we've imprinted the broader culture's self-understanding through our relentless experimentations and our restless improvisations. As Du Bois said in 1903, in *The Souls of Black Folk*, it's a strange thing to see ourselves through the prism of another world. Now we flip the script. Now America, and indeed the globe, sees itself through the prism of blackness. Now our narratives, stories, dispositions, moods, inquiries, preoccupations become the stuff through which people begin to un-derstand themselves—sometimes to their chagrin and sometimes to their celebration.

Metaphorically speaking, black home spaces, which are externalized, now become global resting places for other people. After all, folk from Japan to Frankfurt have adopted black styles and experimented with black cul-tural forms like hip hop. Blackness has become a metaphorical home for people who are seeking self-defi-nition in the midst of a global culture of flux and stretch and process and flow. And if flux and stretch and process and flow are the means by which some forms of technol-ogy are taking off and mediating content, then what's happening is that the larger society is simply tapping back into what black folk have done from the get-go.

That's why it's highly ironic that we straddle some-thing of a digital divide along the super information highway—the tropes, metaphors, and symbols in techno-logical spheres owe an unacknowledged debt to black cul-ture. Heck, even outer space ain't immune from our influence. In an interview with culture critic Kelefa San-neh in the journal *Transition*, hip hop artist Killah Priest, of the hip hop collective Wu Tang Clan, responded to Sanneh's question about why he rapped about outer space so much. Killah Priest said, "Because that's where we're from! Black people come from space. When you look at the sky, it's black. Without sunlight, forget it: it's black. In the beginning, there was darkness." The universe is our home because the universe's sense of home is connected to its blackness, and therefore to our blackness.

So it's coming full circle. The question is: Do black people have the ability to tap into the political and economic success of cultures that they, at least indirectly, helped to birth? Usually we're on the losing end of the proposition; we're usually exploited in some form or fashion, because we are largely consumers at that level. Even though the production of those cultures derives from our own ideals and identities, we usually don't, to twist Karl Marx's phrase, own the means of protection. And that's why, ironically enough, we are both the producers and consumers of identities that originated within, or were inspired by, our own culture.

I'm that nice son / f--- Michaelangelo,
I'm Michael Eric Dyson / slice 'em like a viking.

—**Black Thought of The Roots, "Thought Is Like Freestyle"**

TRACK 2.

"THIS DARK DICTION HAS BECOME AMERICA'S ADDICTION"

CREDITS

Guest Artist: *Meta DuEwa Jones*

Label: *University of Texas at Austin*

Studio Location: *Austin and Philadelphia*

Year Recorded: *2006*

Samples: *Jacques Derrida * Peter Linebaugh * Amilcar Cabral * Avery Johnson * Paul Gilroy * Nas * Jay-Z * Kanye West * Earl Graves * Ralph Waldo Emerson*

Shout Outs: *Rhetorical Genius * The Projects * The Black Diaspora * The Black Atlantic * Global Influence of Hip Hop * Blood Diamonds*

Head Nods: *Jay-Z * Nas * Kanye West * Common * Talib Kweli * Ice Cube * Russell Simmons * Jermaine Dupri * Diddy*

TRACK 2.

"THIS DARK DICTION HAS BECOME AMERICA'S ADDICTION"

Language, Diaspora, and Hip Hop's Bling Economy

Meta DuEwa Jones: When you consider the intellectual ingenuity of hip hop artists, you are describing rhetorical genius rooted in a black aesthetic. It shouldn't surprise anybody to learn that Talib Kweli or Kanye West or Common all have mothers who received their doctorates. Or as Kanye West says in "Hey Mama," "Mama told me to go to school git your doctorate / something to fall back on you could profit with / but still supported me when I did the opposite." Far from being in contradiction to an authentic tradition in African American culture, it is the inevitable extension of it.

Michael Eric Dyson: What you said is absolutely right. The fact that three of the most gifted rappers come from highly educated mothers—Dr. Brenda Green is Talib Kweli's mother, Dr. Donda West is Kanye West's mother, and Dr. Mahalia Ann Hines is Common's mother— doesn't detract from their authenticity in my mind. Perhaps the opportunity that flowed from their lower-middle-class existence gave them perspective on the horrors they witnessed. None of these geniuses were by any means rich, so they were close enough to the ghetto to narrate the truth of what they witnessed, and maybe even lived. And that doesn't necessarily exist over against what Tupac saw as a poor child who lived in a homeless shelter, who moved several times, and whose mother was a crack addict and a deeply intelligent woman. But he also saw other stories and truths as all great artists do.

But here's the surpassing irony: what you said is true not only for young folk we expect to be literate because they've been nurtured in homes where that value has been transmitted, but it's also true of a lot of young folk with genius who weren't reared in the homes of formally well-educated parents.

For instance, Nas is an eighth-grade dropout from the Queensbridge Projects in Queens, who happens to be one of the most fiercely gifted lyricists in the history of hip hop. Sure, his father, Olu Dara, is a talented musician who split from Nas's mother when Nas was thirteen, but not even the advantage of his father's gifts can fully account for Nas's rhetorical genius. Nas summarizes his rhetorical raison d'être when he spits one of his earliest verses:

> It's only right that I was born to use mics,
> and the stuff that I write, it's even tougher than dice
> I'm takin' rapping to a new plateau through rap slow
> My rhyming is a vitamin held without a capsule.

Tupac had an incredibly insightful mother, a social revolutionary and Black Panther who struggled with crack addiction, who made him read the *New York Times* from cover to cover for punishment. Tupac was a high school dropout, but his rhetorical genius, his speaking from the heart through a prolific and potent pen, is undeniable. Jay-Z hailed from Brooklyn's Marcy Projects, Scarface came from Houston's infamous Fifth Ward, and both of them are rhetorical geniuses. So you have to think of these unlikely bearers of a noble verbal tradition when you think about the use of rhetoric to defend degraded black youth, for whom rhetoric becomes the sound of a social reveille.

The best of these rhetoricians, in their social and artistic functions, have a great deal in common with some of the greatest rhetoricians ever. One thinks about

Shakespeare or Chaucer or the writer of the Decameron. One thinks about Melvin Tolson, or Langston Hughes, or Nikki Giovani, or Sonia Sanchez. One thinks about Walt Whitman.

Jones: Or Rita Dove.

Dyson: Exactly right. One thinks about all these great rhetorical traditions from multiple strands. One thinks about Yeats or Rilke. One thinks about a whole range of poetic meters and inventions and rhythms and tonalities. One thinks of Yosef Koumunyakaa, Elizabeth Alexander, and Jane Cortez, or Thomas Sayers Ellis experimenting with the beat of go-go music in his poetic meter. So when you think about all this, the amazing thing is that these young rhetoricians are denied the legitimacy of their accomplishment because we pathologize them on a moral level. The moral qualms of a bourgeois class have obscured the genius of their own children who, like jazz artists, have to go foreign before they become familiar. They have to go global before they find local appeal. We saw this with the magazines. Before rappers were put on the cover of black magazines they were put on the cover of white magazines. Before they were featured on BET, they were on MTV. So they had to go away before they could come home.

We often speak about home as a metaphor in black life. The intense "de-homing" of our own children—the challenge to their domestic tranquility within the confines of our moral worldviews—is, metaphorically speaking, a form of child abuse. It's a way to retroactively abort the seminal sources of black rhetorical genius. The tragedy is that we have failed to come to grips with the enormous achievement of our own children, because we're so angry at them. The larger world embraces them in ways we've failed to do, collectively, within our race.

I'm not suggesting we can't be critically engaged with our children's aesthetic expression. But how can we be effectively engaged if we don't know what we're engaging with? We don't have to romanticize our young rhetorical artists to appreciate them. Our moral traditions may lead us to repudiate most of what the worst of them do while applauding much of what the best of them do. The problem is we don't know how to make those distinctions, and a large part of not knowing how is bound up with our ethical aversion to the style these rhetoricians adopt. There's a way to be seriously critical—after all, folk who know and love hip hop manage to do it—and still appreciate the sheer magnitude of talent that characterizes the best of pavement poetry.

And what these young folk do with the language is nothing short of remarkable. They don't simply replicate what they've been given; they stretch it out, break some of it off, reconstitute it, and prove that literary critic Jacques Derrida is right, that we "only ever have one language" that is "not at one with itself." We have a plurality of voices and rhetoric, and there's "no such thing as *a* language." We should practice linguistic humility—and not rhetorical condescension—and be mindful of our children's sheer verbal wizardry and inventiveness.

Jones: Much has been made of the global dissemination of hip hop in Cuba, Ghana, London, and Jamaica, for example, and its fusion with world music, Afro-beat, reggae, and so forth. How would you characterize the relationship between hip hop and other expressive cultural forms throughout the African diaspora?

Dyson: The origins of hip hop have always been informed by Afro-diasporic elements. The black Atlantic—a phrase that captures how the meanings and identities of blackness travel back and forth across oceans, cultures, tribes, traditions, languages, and nations—is writ large on the rhetorical styles and the sonic fury of hip hop from the beginning. When we tell the story about DJ Kool Herc coming here from the Caribbean, we must highlight the transatlantic navigation of black identities.

Although hip hop had its African American artistic womb in the Bronx, we know its narrative of origins ranges far beyond those borders. When we're talking hip hop, we're already speaking about black diaspora. We're already talking about the black Atlantic, before the brilliant Peter Linebaugh wrote about it, and before—what's my man's name?—Paul Gilroy, who has written brilliantly about the black Atlantic but missed some indigenous African American moments in his harsh and crude readings of the black diaspora.

The black diaspora is nowhere better exemplified than in the incredible fusion of multiple languages engaged in the rhetorical, rhythmic, percussive, tonal, and sonic structures of hip hop. Even a brief listen to hip hop gives you a sense of its sheer musical vitality and tonal signatures: the polyrhythmic structure of hip hop cadences, like the funk music it partially bit off; the improvisational elements of the art form; the booming and bracing sound systems being transported from the Caribbean to American soil; the guttural cries, shrieks, and moans that lace the aural landscape; and the ingenious multicultural dimensions of rhetoric insinuated into the percussive elements of African diasporic cultures.

Even before we consider empirically how hip hop has been globally indexed and internationally consumed, whether in Brazil, where hip hop is flourishing, or in Cuba and in Germany, where it has also taken root, there are anecdotal ways we can track its huge influence. I think of a story I recently heard where, during the 2006 NBA finals, Dallas Mavericks Coach Avery Johnson wanted to get his team away from the distractions of Miami—they were playing the Miami Heat in their arena, but family members had tagged along, the custom in the finals. So Johnson took his team to a hotel in Ft. Lauderdale, to a spot more than thirty minutes outside of the city, with instructions not to leave the property.

Johnson also made each of the teammates have roommates. One of the more interesting pairings occurred with seven-foot forward Dirk Nowitzki, who is a white German, and the black American six-foot-one veteran point guard Darrell Armstrong, nicknamed "Black College" because he attended Fayetteville State, a historically black college in North Carolina. Armstrong said that all they did during their time together was watch soccer and listen to German hip hop. Now haven't things come full circle when a white guy from Germany is schooling a brother from America on the intricacies of international hip hop! Hip hop is global in that sense as well.

What this illustrates is how the black diaspora really begins to color even European cultural moments. It begins to colonize what is usually the colonizer. It begins to reappropriate and recolonize voices and sources and identities far from its shores of influence. There are multiple meanings, operating simultaneously, by which the black diaspora can be referenced. The moments of black diaspora within hip hop are by now diachronic—occurring across different time periods—*and* synchronic—happening in many places at the same time. When you talk about hip hop's global distribution, you have to talk about what's going on with reggaeton, Afro-beat, and jazz, especially in England, and the different expressions occurring in Cuba and Bahia. Hip hop is a language that travels across local borders internationally and finds resonant rhetorical uses in strange places.

For instance, when Solidarity was legalized in Poland in 1989, some Polish protesters blasted NWA's "F— tha Police" to express their outrage at oppressive social and political forces. These Polish brothers and sisters had likely not been to Compton, but Compton came to them, by means of a sound and a fury and a force that found perfect articulation in lead rapper Ice Cube's vocals. For these Polish citizens, Ice Cube became the iconographic interrogator of state policies of repression. It's something to think that in Poland, at least for a shining moment, the force of terror was interrupted by the sonic blast and the aesthetic articulation of degraded black people subject to state terror through police brutality in America.

In this case, as in so many others, diasporic elements within black American identity are exported and become globally consumed. And interestingly enough, they become instructive for other people, even beyond the black diaspora, to complain about and protest against the limits of freedom. But more particularly, in the question you posed, I think it's important to understand the feistiness of hip hop, the way hip hop is able to renew itself beyond the dead ends of the bling and the booze and the broads when it goes international. Hip hop is able to renew its intellectual identity when it begins to forge alliances with the cultural expression of degraded and oppressed people around the world. Hip hop is enlivened by its edifying fusions with other cultures, other traditions, other peoples who begin to take it up, and who begin to see in its expression an identification with some of the gloom and the glory of their indigenous cultures.

Jones: I'm going to pick up another expression of the diaspora and ask you to reflect on lessons from "within the bling," as you have said, when it goes international. Consider Kanye West and Jay-Z's collaboration on the song "Diamonds from Sierra Leone," with its explicit critique of violence within the diamond trade diasporically:

> Good morning this ain't Vietnam. Still / People lose
>   hands, legs, arms, for real
> Then it was known as Sierra Leone / And how it
>   connects to the diamonds we own . . .

The song continues in a manner that fuses the iconography of the bling in hip hop locally with the ethical quandary of acknowledging that globally, other black bodies are severed in the service of the bling. That's another kind of diasporic manifestation of hip hop, isn't it?

Dyson: That's a very powerful point. I think it's marvelous that, within the political economy of the bling, there shines a luminous moment of critical self-inventory and cultural interrogation, not just self-consciousness. Remember Kanye said on his first album, "We're all self-conscious, I'm just the first to admit it." So it makes sense that Kanye would be the artist to take up this cause and engage with the black diaspora in one of its more nefarious moments: the appropriation of African labor at violent cost to life and limb, as African American millionaires across the waters celebrate a gaudily excessive lifestyle fueled by the suffering and death of their kin slaving in caves thousands of miles away.

And since Kanye was a figure who celebrated such a lifestyle, he's committing a kind of Amilcar Cabral–like class suicide—just to keep the theme of Africa going here, and its influence throughout the black diaspora—by asking serious questions about the cultivation and distribution of "blood diamonds." This is as serious a question as you can ask on a four-minute pop record. From inside the arc of the diamond desire of hip hop's bling economy, Kanye spits some truth that links him to the black diaspora in edifying fashion. It gets beyond another element he's also celebrated: diamonds as a mark of social status and phallic displacement. You know, mine's bigger than yours; mine's shinier than yours.

Jones: And harder.

Dyson: Oh, absolutely, we'll go all the way: harder, sharper, flintier, and the like. Of course, another dimension of this has to be commented on for its diasporic angle, but not one that's pretty. Russian immigrant Yakov "Jacob the Jeweler" Arabov is damn near an icon to hip hop's bling royalty and is cited on many rap records. He's probably the major distributor of diamonds, arguably making him one of the cocreators of the political economy of bling. Arabov has been accused of laundering something like $270 million for notorious street gang Black Mafia Family as well as attempting to distribute more than 400 kilograms of cocaine.

You might say that's a black eye for hip hop, but I find it an irresistible angle to note this may be the underside of hip hop's international appeal, so that folk with bad intentions can exploit young folk or join forces with horrible elements within hip hop. And Jacob the Jeweler's presence points to a nonblack person who co-created a moment of seminal, if problematic, productivity within African American culture—the reproduction of the bling ideology. Furthermore, the diamond iconography registers as a moment of black authenticity when diamonds are explicitly external to the culture. It can't be associated with black authenticity except as rich rappers consume these diamonds as extensions of their economic vitality and their virility: the harder and bigger my diamond, the harder and bigger my influence.

Of course, what's interesting about the remix to "Diamonds" is Jay-Z's verse, arguably the cleverest line on an already clever album, where he spits: "I'm not a businessman, I'm a *business*, man / So let me handle my business damn." I don't have the time to break down all of the possible literary meanings and cultural readings of this fertile line, but at the very least we see Jay-Z attempting to articulate a political aesthetic of entrepreneurship, where there's a battle of nouns. In Jay-Z's mouth, business sounds more like a verb, functions more as an action than a denominator of a person, place, or thing. Jay-Z sees himself as a business to be invested in and expanded, and he's taken hustling savvy and corporate smarts (hence the commercial celebrating him as the "CEO of hip hop") to the next level. So all of it I think operates simultaneously within the context of current hip hop.

Jones: Your remarks indicate a willingness to see in hip hop's future an approach to its corporatism that is more complex than dichotomies between underground and commercial rap music. Is there a way to acknowledge hip hop's burgeoning commercial strength without its ethic being compromised?

Dyson: Sure there is. I recently sat on a panel addressing The Crisis of Black Men with legendary businessman Earl Graves, founder of *Black Enterprise* magazine, and a very dear friend of mine. But he began the panel by showing a picture, dated, I suspect, circa 1986, at the height of the Run DMC era, featuring rappers with gold chains around their necks. Graves held up the picture and said, and I'm paraphrasing, "This is the stuff we're trying to get away from."

And then he showed a picture of young black men in suits and ties, circa 1965, and pronounced, "This is what we're trying to get back to." Despite the obvious anachronism of getting after young folk with outdated pictures—underscoring how culturally out of touch a lot of our beloved elders are—I couldn't resist retorting, "Mr. Graves, hip hop tonight is not having a panel whose aim is to try to become successful in entrepreneurship, as this conference is trying to do. Many of them are *already* there."

Remember Jay-Z's quote about being a business. Besides that, thousands of young black professionals eat from hip hop's table, in the sense that it has provided spin-off spaces in corporate America for lawyers, managers, accountants, and the like, who handle a hip hop clientele. I said to Mr. Graves, "After all, you're an incredible entrepreneur, and if you're about entrepreneurs, you've got to be about opening up space for these young African American men and women so that they can leverage their authority in ways that you pointed to, because you inspired many of them. And some of them, like Jay-Z, have taken it to the next level." He replied that "Nobody with tattoos on their body or low-slung pants can tell me anything."

And the tragedy is that Jay-Z, Russell Simmons, Jermaine Dupri, Diddy, Master P, and a whole bunch of other cats who've seized corporate America *on their own terms* are dismissed. Of course, most of those cats dress in very expensive suits as well, and know how to code-switch and, as Jay-Z said in one of his songs, "change clothes." And now, because of an older generation's aesthetic revulsion to the iconography of hip hop—the ink on the body, the clothes on the body, the culturally consumed bodies that have been overly interpreted and therefore now hide beneath prison-inspired clothing—we miss out on our own children's genius. Again! Then we blame white folk for exploiting hip hop by forcing our kids to rap about cars and women, more than freedom and spirit.

Some of that is certainly true, maybe even a lot of it, but older black folk must assume responsibility for turning their back on hip hop at its beginning. Now they expect a genre and generation that they dissed to bow down at their feet. It's like an absent parent returning home to rule the roost after he or she abandoned the children. But the dynamics have changed: the kids are grown and successful. So thanks, but no thanks. You can surely understand that mind-set from many young artists.

Naturally enough, young artists turned to white folk, who in large part own the means of production. Beyond that, some of these white record executives were able to spot, and exploit, our kids' talents in ways that many black folk refused to do. I don't want to paint them as saints, but neither can I paint them as demons. Some of them genuinely got what our kids were trying to say and do. And we must acknowledge that it's not a simple either/or—either you sell out to white corporate interests and get exploited, or you stay pure and black and at home and undistributed and unable to cross over.

By the way, that's a huge difference between black generations. Civil rights folk said, "We'll dress up and play the rules the white way and cross over." Hip hop seized the reins of its destiny and insisted that it make music its way, and white folk could cross over to them. They concluded that, like Emerson said, they'd made a superior product, and the world would beat a path to their door. They felt they'd make the white folk dress and talk like them—and we know, at least among their kids, they've been quite successful.

But there is another way: become entrepreneurs, learn the record *business*, and retain your roots. Remember that roots are meant to nourish, not strangle. But you can maintain your integrity—God yes, even your authenticity, though it's a much more complicated matter than living in the hood or speaking a certain way—and still be successful. You can spit venom at white supremacy, social injustice, the personal limitations imposed by a dominant culture, and still use—contrary to the great Audre Lorde—the master's tools to dismantle the master's house or at least break in and enjoy some of the bounty.

I mean, listen to Jay-Z:

Now you know yo' ass is Willie/When they got you in a
    mag/For like half a billi
And your ass ain't Lilly/White
That mean that shit you write must be illy/Either that
    or your flow is silly
It's both
I don't mean to boast/But damn if I don't brag
Them crackers gonna act like I ain't on they ass
The Martha Stewart/That's far from Jewish
Far from a Harvard student/Just had the balls to do it
And no I'm not through with it/In fact I'm just
    previewin' it
This ain't the show I'm just EQ'in it/One, two and I
    won't stop abusin' it
To groupie girls stop false accusin' it/Back to the music
The Maybach roof is translucent/Niggas got a problem
    Houston
What up B/They can't shut up me/Shut down I
Not even P.E./I'mma ride
God forgive me for my brash delivery
But I remember vividly/What these streets did to me
So picture me/Lettin' these clowns nit pick at me
Paint me like a pickiny.

These verses capture for me the intense development
of the entrepreneur's spirit that takes us back before Mar-
cus Garvey and down to Ken Chenault at American Ex-

press. Except Jay-Z can still use "cracker" as a term for white supremacist corporate capitalism, even as he forges strategic alliances with the people who dominate that culture, for the purpose of defending his black brothers and sisters. I'll take a Jay-Z over a Bill Cosby, at least the Cosby who's recently emerged as a bitter curmudgeon. Bill Cosby lacks the courage to speak against the white corporate capitalists who bolster his economic stability as he beats up on poor black people, while Jay-Z talks about his personal and social responsibility while defending the socially vulnerable whose backs are against the wall.

> These are our heroes . . . some real folks with clout /
> Tavis Smiley, Michael Eric Dyson /
> Stokely Carmichael, let's try to be like them.
>
> —*Nas, "These Are Our Heroes"*

TRACK 3.

"IT'S TRENDY TO BE THE CONSCIOUS MC"

CREDITS

Guest Artist: *Thomas Gibson*

Label: *QDIII Productions*

Studio Location: *Los Angeles*

Year Recorded: *2004*

Samples: *Amiri Baraka * Public Enemy * Robin D.G. Kelley * Mos Def * Claude Levi-Strauss * Lauryn Hill * Outkast * Paul Simon * Joe DiMaggio * Gary Webb * Mike Davis * Kool Moe Dee * Frederick Douglass * Lena Horne*

Shout Outs: *Black Arts Movement (BAM) * Social Struggle * Hip Hop Origins * Commercialism * Caribbean Culture * Reaganism * Thatcherism * Conscious Hip Hop * Generational Conflict * Crack Economy*

Head Nods: *Nas * Public Enemy * Common * Talib Kweli * KRS-ONE * Boogie Down Productions * X-Clan * A Tribe Called Quest * 2Pac * Mos Def * Bahamadia * Lauryn Hill * The Coup * Dead Prez * DJ Kool Herc * Kurtis Blow * Run DMC * Will Smith * DJ Jazzy Jeff and the Fresh Prince * MC Lyte * D-Nice * Kool Moe Dee * Doug E. Fresh * Heavy-D * J-Live * The Roots * Black Star * De La Soul * Ice Cube * Gang Starr * Immortal Technique * Slick Rick * Ras Kass*

"IT'S TRENDY TO BE THE CONSCIOUS MC"

Culture, Rhetoric, Crack, and the Politics of Rap

Thomas Gibson: If we are to truly understand the meaning of so-called conscious hip hop, we must place it in relationship to older black cultural arts movements, especially during the 1960s. Can you discuss the relationship between the black arts movement and contemporary politically motivated hip hop?

Michael Eric Dyson: There's no question that the most gifted figures in the Black Arts Movement [BAM], including Larry Neal, Addison Gayle, Hoyt Fuller, Amiri

Baraka, Nikki Giovanni, and Sonia Sanchez, understood that politics is central to artistic vision. The Black Arts Movement, whose defining decade lasted from 1965 to 1975, contended that there is a close relationship between morality and aesthetics, especially the black aesthetic that its advocates believed was generated from the politics and history of black freedom struggles. BAM also argued that cultural nationalism is the basis for a distinct black cultural identity in the social sphere. BAM members held that the politics of black power reflect and guide the artistic vision of black culture. BAM also argued the strong tie between artist and community, spurning the heroic individualism of European models of artistic endeavor in favor of the collective roots of artists who express the values, beliefs, ideals, and perceptions of the communities to which they belong.

For the members of the Black Arts Movement, there was no such thing as a serious artist who was not concerned about the social struggles for self-determination and political liberty of their people, struggles which in large part inspired their art. So the participants in the Black Arts Movement were persuaded of the need to fuse politics, art, and community. Several questions guided their agenda: How are the arts serving the broader black world? How does art imply and forge political cohesion among the black masses? How does the Black Arts Movement help to revolutionize or fundamentally transform the consciousness of ordinary people and move them from anger to action? Art was never far from life, never artificially divorced from suffering or celebration. It was always found at the intersection of reflection and reaction or of critical consciousness and social intervention. Art was a servant of the masses.

When it comes to similarities between hip hop and the Black Arts Movement, we're talking about different time periods, with different artistic constraints and different political and racial situations. In the 1960s and 1970s, black folk were struggling for the sorts of political freedoms and economic opportunities that the most fortunate members of the young black generation now take for granted. But there are parallels.

For instance, in BAM there was a great effort to make literature accessible to everyday black folk, especially through live poetry performances. BAM also brought art to the masses through the plays of figures like Ed Bullins, who penned *In the Wine Time*, and Amiri Baraka, who wrote *Dutchman*. Bullins's work led to the founding of the New Lafayette Theatre (NLT), and Baraka's play helped establish the Black Arts Repertory Theatre/School (BART/S), the institutional fruit of BAM's ideological and intellectual vision. The visual art of the Black Arts Movement was intended to demystify the esoteric meanings and abstract images of experimental Afro-expressionism, rooting it instead in the aesthetic imperatives of black resistance and liberation—from Ademola Olugebefola's 1968 work, *Space Dance,* to Lev T. Mills's 1972 collage *I'm Funky, But Clean.* I'd say rap, especially in its earlier incarnations, when it was directly connected to relatively intimate spaces of recreation, leisure, and cultural creativity, was fueled by the same energy and purpose as BAM's live poetry readings.

And graffiti artists—like the legendary Fab Five Freddy, who helped spread the art form—with their aerosol cans in hand, were literally painting themselves into existence on the walls of American cities in the name of a vernacular aesthetic that reflected the designs of ordinary life. During the golden age of hip hop, from 1987 to 1993, Afrocentric and black nationalist rap were prominent. Thus rap and graffiti measured the artistic weight of real black and brown youth who were largely invisible and unheard.

Conscious rap—or rap that is socially aware and consciously connected to historic patterns of political protest and aligned with progressive forces of social critique—owes a debt, whether its artists realize it or not, to the Black Arts Movement. Artists like KRS-1 and Boogie Down Productions, Public Enemy, X-Clan, A Tribe Called Quest—and more recently 2Pac, Talib Kweli, Common, Mos Def, Bahamadia, Lauryn Hill, The Coup, Dead Prez, and Nas—have infused their art with varying forms of political awareness. They have also occasionally linked their work to quests for social justice, whether making a song to galvanize social response to police brutality or to dramatize and inspire social outrage against an unjust war. At the height of politically conscious rap, during hip hop's golden age, groups like Public Enemy depended on a kind of racial and political literacy for folk to grasp what they were saying.

For instance, that incendiary line from Public Enemy's monumental jam, "Fight the Power": "Elvis was a hero to most, but he never meant sh— to me / Straight up racist, the sucker was simple and plain / Motherf— him and John Wayne." That couplet distills incredible fury against the appropriation of black culture by white figures like Presley, and delivers a rebuke to the corrosive racial politics of an All-American icon like Wayne. Like their Black Arts Movement predecessors, conscious rappers insist that politics, art, and life are intricately intertwined. One of the clearest examples of such a link among BAM members is Amiri Baraka's controversial poem "Black Art," where he wails, "Poems are bullshit unless they are teeth or trees or lemons piled / on a step. Or black ladies dying / of men leaving nickel hearts / beating them down. F— poems . . . / We want 'poems that kill.' / Assassin poems, Poems that shoot / guns. Poems that wrestle cops into alleys / and take their weapons leaving them dead."

The Black Arts Movement owed its existence to social struggle in the larger political landscape where black folk were arguing over unequal educational resources, social and economic inequality, continuing white supremacy, and more subtle forms of racial injustice. The political rap of the late 1980s and early 1990s reflected renewed forms of racial solidarity and social protest—the popular reappearance of the image and ideas of Malcolm X, the rise of black neonationalism, and the emergence of a racially aware, politically engaged era in black film, led by Spike Lee. Contemporary conscious rappers are lauded as much for what they *don't* say as for what they spit on record. They don't brag about exorbitant jewelry, excessive women, or expensive automobiles. Conscious rappers *do* talk about racial injustice, police brutality, over-incarceration, political prisoners, rampant poverty, radical educational inequality and more.

A critical difference between the Black Arts Movement and conscious rap is that hip hop has not been supported by a vibrant political movement. Although many younger figures are politically active, today's artists have a more difficult time identifying with any particular movement, since there's been a severe diminution of social resistance and political rebellion. There have been keen political moments—Al Sharpton's mobilizations around police brutality cases, the revival of black nationalist community activism, the presidential runs by Jesse Jackson in 1984 and 1988—but there has been nothing like the concerted effort at social resistance, racial uplift, and political engagement as occurred in the 1960s and early 1970s.

That suggests a few points. First, the relentless assault on young blacks for being apolitical and socially apathetic is also an indictment of the broader black culture, which was similarly inactive. We've got to resist the temptation to romanticize the 1960s; there was only a small fraction of black folk who hit the streets during the black freedom struggles. Second, there's a problem far beyond the political failure of hip hop. There is also a failure of black political imagination among black elites and other activists who might spark social movement.

Third, generations of artists owe a great deal of their social consciousness and activist energy to larger political forces at work in the culture. While black music at its best has often supplied a supplementary argument for political change, it is not a substitute for actual politics. And if you don't have a vital political movement, the music can only go so far. It can *help* alter the mind-set of the masses; it can *help* create awareness of the need for social change; it can *help* dramatize injustice; and it can *help* articulate the disenchantment of significant segments of the citizenry. But it cannot alone transform social relations and political arrangements. Politically charged music can *reinforce* important social values, but it cannot *establish* them.

It's unfair to charge hip hop with a political failure that it was not accountable for to begin with. That's like holding Curtis Mayfield, who sang "Keep on Pushin'," accountable for the failure of the late phase, northern-based arm of the civil rights movement in the late 1960s, or holding James Brown, who sang "I'm Black and I'm

Proud," responsible for the failure of the black power struggle in the early 1970s.

It's a mistake for folk who are singing or rapping about political matters—as important as that is, especially in our era when traditional politics is a hard sell to youth— to believe that what they're doing is a substitute for social struggle and political engagement. Of course, we've got to acknowledge an expanded, more nuanced conception of politics—and I agree wholeheartedly with historian Robin D. G. Kelley's brilliant discussion in his book *Race Rebels* of the infrapolitics, or veiled forms of political behavior, that are often hidden from public view. Too often, complex forms of social activity and political resistance that don't fit into narrow notions of politics are either ignored or dismissed. But arguments about the just distribution of resources are still an important political behavior. In this sense, hip hop is an extension of, not a substitute for, a tradition, even as I think that hip hop has sparked a compelling brand of political activism that joins aesthetic expression and social awareness.

To be sure, in an age of diminished political expectation, eroded social engagement, and disenchantment with government, the politics of hip hop are to be welcomed and celebrated. After all, aesthetic expression can have a strong bearing on political understanding for a generation that gets its news from Jon Stewart's *The Daily Show*. Many politically astute rappers offer brilliant commentary on everything from war to racism. Many socially conscious rappers are understandably nervous with the term "conscious rapper" because it segregates them from the broader body of hip hop. Moreover, the term can be used to set them up as "better" or "more enlightened," which most understandably want to avoid. And the term can be used to deny them complexity and variety, the hallmarks of robust art. After all, even conscious rappers may want to brag, party, and make love.

Think of Mos Def's astute analysis of how the media frames black males accused of wrongdoing, while going easy on white men accused of similar offenses. In his "Mr. Nigga," Mos Def raps:

> You can laugh and criticize Michael Jackson if you
> wanna
> Woody Allen molested and married his stepdaughter
> Same press kicking dirt on Michael's name
> Show Woody and Soon-Yi at the playoff game (holding
> hands)
> Sit back and just bug, think about that
> Would he get that type of dap if his name was Woody
> Black?
> O.J. was found innocent by a jury of his peers
> And they been f— with that nigga for the last 5 years
> Is it fair, is it equal, is it just, is it right?
> Do you do the same sh— when the defendant's face is
> white?
> If white boy's doing well its success

If I start doing well its suspect . . .
They say they want you successful, but then they make
   it stressful
You start keeping pace, they start changing up the
   tempo.

At their best, socially conscious rappers tackle thorny social problems and perhaps inspire those who engage in action. Such a role for the artist should not be downplayed, underestimated, or even undervalued.

There's got to be a division of labor that recognizes the talents that each person possesses, although those of us who are fortunate enough to have greater amounts of leisure, labor flexibility, social support, and cultural recognition are held to a higher standard. In a sense, we are more responsible to the common good. As we say in Christian circles, "To whom much is given, much is required." But everyone must use their talents and gifts to the best of their ability to make political struggle and social change work. It's not a matter of hierarchy, rank, and privilege, but shared responsibility by all—though some have more responsibility than others. The lessons of the 1960s remind us that ordinary people—and often very young people—fought valiantly for the social change they needed.

Everyone should participate in social change, from the shoe shine man to the state representative, from the beautician to the boxer. That means it's not fair to single out young folk as being more responsible for social change than others, especially poor young folk who are doing the best they can after being abandoned by their more prosperous elders. And some of them have also been written off by society as pathological or useless. Of course, not everyone can lead a march, though everybody can join one. Not everyone can write books, though all of us who can read should teach those who can't read to read for themselves, while we all become more literate about social issues. Not all of us can sing or dance well, but all of us can sing our own songs, dance our own dances, and support artists whose views reflect our values. Artists play a critical role in doing what they do, and if they do more than that, it's a blessing, bonus, and boon.

Gibson: If young people recalled the origins of rap, could it help to stimulate their awareness of hip hop's broader cultural and political meaning and use?

Dyson: Absolutely. The origins of rap are black and Latino. And it wasn't simply a matter of African American youth, but black folk throughout the diaspora. DJ Kool Herc came over from the Caribbean, transporting with him that booming sound system that was common in particular spaces in West Indian culture. That revolutionized and reshaped the sonic landscape in the Bronx, the birthplace of hip hop. It was here that the four central elements of hip hop emerged: break dancing, DJ-ing (or turntablism), graffiti, and rapping. Hip hop was broad and open, and from the start, already looking beyond a single black culture. Some of its earliest artists expressed concern about the racial struggles and social and political conditions of young black folk. Even rappers known primarily for fun and partying in rap's golden age also embraced racial and political consciousness. Kurtis Blow's "The Breaks," for instance, showed his awareness of the bad breaks black folk got—and literally played on, and off of, in their moral and musical lives—while Run DMC's "It's Like That" proved their consciousness of black history and their connection to a tradition of black social struggle.

The various genres and approaches in rap music weren't nearly as segregated as they are now. In the present musical circumstance, there are big barriers between conscious and political rap, gangsta rap, materialistic rap (or bling hop), hardcore Bohemian, and varieties of geographically identified and regionally driven hip hop, from southern "crunk" to West Coast rap. But "back in the day," on the same bill you'd have the Will Smith-led DJ Jazzy Jeff and the Fresh Prince, a humorous, family-friendly rap duo, and Public Enemy with its incendiary and controversial political themes. So you'd hear "Charlie Mack Is the First out the Limo" and "Fight the Power" in the same show.

Hip hop took root in a culture of hardship. Even the technology that played such a crucial role in rap's origins derived from hardship. Many black and brown kids in vocational school were sent to work repairing the turntables for rich suburban school kids. But that circumstance drove their experimentation with various technological forms to undergird hip hop's aesthetic expansion. So these young folk ended up putting turntables next to each other, and out of that emerged the practice of cuing up one record while the other one is playing, and you're listening to it, finding the exact spot to extend and repeat the break beat through scratching, and eventually with looping.

When hip hop started, the DJ had control and rocked the party through his sonic play and technical experimentalism. Look how it happened on the ground: what was essentially an attempt to repair broken turntables was used to generate an alternative sonic culture full of technological innovation that supposedly ignorant black and brown folk have now turned into a billion-dollar industry. Anthropologists call it *bricolage*, a French term first used by Claude Lévi-Strauss to mean using what is literally at hand to create something—a style, an approach, a practice. So these young black and brown folk took the technological leftovers of a richer consumer culture and fashioned a cultural and musical expression that has lasted to this day.

But they were also driven to create something important out of the fragments of culture because of the economic suffering of poor folk during the Reagan era.

Resources were sparse, especially in the inner-city schools targeted by cruel budget cuts that depleted arts programs and denied poor children access to instruments and broad musical literacy. So when older folk, especially musicians, complain that young folk don't play instruments, they must realize that there's hardly support for young folk learning to play the saxophone, or the clarinet, or the trumpet, or the drums, because those are aesthetic artifacts of a bygone musical era when the opportunity to deepen one's musical vocabulary was far greater. But the economic exigencies of deprivation forced poor black and brown kids into greater survival and aesthetic creativity. Graffiti was a way of scarring the face of public memory with the incisions of black and brown presence. You want to register who you are.

Break dancing was the attempt to take preexisting forms and movement—especially Brazilian capoeira—and fuse it with New York street style and rearticulate it as an aesthetic measure of identity. It was a way of saying, "I'm going to take the breaks of life and use them creatively." The breaks in the music were taken by the DJs in one direction—expanded and looped to form a new musical expression from an already existing musical form—and in another direction by dancers, who exploit the sonic experimentation with break beats into an eclectic dance practice that fuses a variety of ethnic and stylistic gestures. The break—something relatively minor in the musical arsenal—has now been highlighted and, within the aural logic of hip hop, made a major aesthetic and creative element. A lot of things in early hip hop were like chitlins—the stuff that was largely cast away, but then poor folk took hold of it and made it a dynamic part of the musical diet.

That survival habit—of turning pork bellies into desirable menu items and eventually big business as commodities on the futures market—grew out of a culture of political and social suffering. It reminds us that politics is not only what we hear in hip hop lyrics, but it's also in the aesthetic and technical forms that derive from the cultural and intellectual imperatives of restless black innovation. This brings us back to the beginning of hip hop and back to DJ Kool Herc. One of the important lessons we can take from Kool Herc's pioneering role in hip hop's sound is how transatlantic blackness—a blackness that is not understood in relationship to any one terrain or geography but in how they intersect and interact along a number of intellectual and aesthetic routes—was at work from the very beginning of hip hop culture.

Transatlantic blackness also shows up in the struggles of black folk for relative artistic autonomy and racial freedom from the oppressive, archconservative political narratives of Thatcherism in England and Reaganism in the United States. In America, such suffering fueled an art form that borrowed elements of black expression from folk in the Caribbean who also had a vibrant intellectual and artistic back-and-forth with black British culture and ideas. So both the forms and the content of hip hop from the outset were deeply imprinted with profound political meanings. At its best, hip hop gained conscience and caught fire as a result of trying to make commentary on what it saw around it, and by expressing it in the musical idioms and aesthetic conventions that derived from the vibrant intersections of black cultures across many borders.

Gibson: Speak a bit about how politically conscious rappers use their rhetorical gifts to inspire and inform the people who listen to them.

Dyson: Words are important, as a means of upward mobility, or as a means to escape suffering, especially by exposing its horrible intrusion into one's group or neighborhood, or to grapple with a white supremacist society that refuses to acknowledge our fundamental humanity. So in that sense, we give big "ups" or "props" to people who use their words to build a way out of the social neglect and hopelessness to which they've been consigned. But in contrast, we can't pretend that the "bling bling," or the materialism, of hip hop culture grew out of nowhere. It springs in part from people being squeezed into economic deprivation and hungering for material emblems, trinkets, symbols, and rewards. The gross materialism of the surrounding culture fuels the desire to bathe in the ocean of opulence that drowns so many Americans.

None of this means that our artists, who at times mindlessly promote the acquisition of things, shouldn't be held to higher artistic account, or that we should dismiss the question of responsibility for the art they make. There's a vibrant tradition of artists—whether in the Black Arts Movement or in the Harlem Renaissance before it with writers like Langston Hughes and Zora Neale Hurston—who helped us become more aware of, and to struggle with, the problems of the "folk" and of the poor. Their art helped black folk to identify, and to cope with, the social misery of African American people. And many musical artists of the past have done the same.

In our own day, there are many artists who recognize the power of art to inform and inspire, to instigate and cajole, to make their constituencies aware of social, moral, spiritual, and intellectual problems—and resources. The very art that points to problems is often a resource to help grapple with them, if for no other reason than it helps us to acknowledge their existence and the need to do something about them. For instance, think of Lauryn Hill, who sings, "I thought our art was supposed to inspire / music is supposed to take us higher." Even before she sang that, she rapped, as part of the group The Fugees, a telling, brilliant line: "Even after all my logic and my theory / I add a motherf— so you ignorant niggas hear me." In short, she is saying, "I'll use cuss words to seduce you into listening to me so you can hear what I have to say." Part of the demand on artists is to meet folk where they are to take them where they think they need to be.

I think in the larger scheme of things, social and political consciousness among segments of the masses, especially among black youth, has been squelched by the downturn of the economy, the political hopelessness bred by exploitative elites, the huge class chasm in black America, and the consequences of a bitter generational divide. There are a lot of older black people beating up on younger black people, even young black artists who are socially responsible and keenly aware of traditions of black social protest. Look what happened with the unfortunate case of the rap duo Outkast being sued in Detroit in 1999 by representatives for Rosa Parks. What does such a move tell our young black people? We constantly lecture them, "Learn your history; we want you to know something about your elders." Outkast did just that. They created a song, "Rosa Parks," on their third album, *Aquemini,* with the legendary activist's name in it, though she appears in their work more as metaphor than historic personage. And for that, they were sued.

One of the reasons for the suit, according to her representatives, is that Rosa Parks was being dishonored and disrespected by her mere appearance on a rap song—one that, interestingly enough, features very little cursing, and one that, if you give a listen, actually employs her as a structure of consciousness-raising in the lyric. Admittedly the fast pace of the song, its southern diction, and its slang ensured that the song, particularly its chorus, was not an easy one to understand, especially for folk over twenty-five. I'm sure well-meaning advisers and guardians for Ms. Parks, thinking they were protecting her name, image, and legacy, acted to stop Outkast from distributing their song. But it was a tragic gesture, especially since Outkast is one of the most sophisticated, socially aware groups in all of hip hop.

If you listen to the chorus, you can catch the subtle allusion to Parks:

Unh, huh, hush that fuss
Everybody move to the back of the bus
Do you wanna bump or slump with us?
We the type of people make the party get crunk.

And if you listen to the first part of the verse spit by Outkast member Andre 3000, you'll notice the literary and symbolic use of Parks:

I met a gypsy and she hipped me to some life game
To stimulate and activate the left and right brain.

What we get from this fragment of the verse, as well as from the chorus, is that Rosa Parks is a metaphor for an enlightened elder, and that she teaches a curious, receptive young person to segregate the bus of life according to the gifted and nongifted, those ready for opportunity and the ill-prepared. Outkast is essentially saying, "All you wack rappers get to the back of the bus, 'cause the real deal is here now."

Of course, living figures, even famous ones, are hardly used to being seen as metaphors. Joe DiMaggio had a similar problem with singer Paul Simon, when he was part of the duo Simon and Garfunkel, and Simon wrote the lyrics, "Where have you gone, Joe DiMaggio? / A nation turns its lonely eyes to you," from the song "Mrs. Robinson" for the soundtrack to the 1960s landmark film, *The Graduate*. When Simon ran into DiMaggio in public, the baseball legend had a few choice words for Simon. "What do you mean where have I gone? I'm still around. I'm selling 'Mr. Coffee.'" You can imagine Simon saying to him, "No, Mr. DiMaggio, you're a metaphor. We're trying to evoke a time in American history when things were relatively simple, and we could understand what the values and visions of American culture were. We knew who our heroes were. Your fifty-six-game hitting streak symbolizes a time of national achievement and remarkable consistency." So I think Rosa Parks suing Outkast is a tragic mistake, the poignant symbol of the yawning abyss that separates black generations.

Or think about how Janet Jackson was dumped from playing Lena Horne in an upcoming biopic of the legendary actress because of the controversy around Nipplegate—where Jackson's nipple (or at least her breast with a sun-shaped nipple shield) was exposed for a nanosecond after being ripped from its bustier by singer Justin Timberlake during their halftime performance at Superbowl 38. Because of that incident, and Jackson's posing as Horne in *Vanity Fair* magazine—which may have appeared to Horne and her camp as mockery—Horne and her daughter Gail Lumet Buckley insisted Jackson be ousted from an ABC TV film about Horne. Allegedly ABC refused the request, but Jackson nevertheless backed out. Ever since Jackson's departure, the project has floundered. How unfortunate is that? Again, besides a conflict of values, this is at heart a generational tiff. After all, Lena Horne, as classy and beautiful as she is, faced her own struggles in the past. In Vincente Minelli's all-black 1943 musical *Cabin in the Sky*, Horne plays sinful seductress Georgia Brown. In fact, one of her scenes was so racy it was cut from the film—a scene where Horne is singing "Ain't It the Truth" in the bath. Had that scene made the film, it might have stirred the kind of controversy generated by Jackson's Nipplegate more than fifty years later.

So many young black people are cut off from the political wisdom they might receive if older black people would sit down and talk to them, teach them, converse with them—and, yes, learn from them. Older folk shouldn't primarily be about beating young folk down. As a member of an in-between generation, I want to use my tongue as a bridge between the civil rights generation—that's why I write books about Martin Luther King Jr.,

Malcolm X, and Marvin Gaye—and the younger generation—which is why I wrote a book about Tupac Shakur.
At its best, hip hop grapples with politics, which is the
art of making arguments over how social resources are
distributed, cultural capital is accumulated, and ideological legitimacy is secured.

We should always take into account the social condition of the young people who speak and pay close attention to what they say. And we have to understand what
political, economic, and social conditions have challenged and shaped their self-understanding. We've got to
wrestle with what they deem important—their social and
moral priorities. Maybe hip hoppers wouldn't talk so
much about material things if we helped give them a
sense of meaning and a means to connect to sustaining
spiritual and moral and intellectual traditions. We can't
hypocritically condemn the younger generation for their
bling and their materialism, especially since those are sta-
ples of American culture. Money is critical to having a
good life in our society. But we want to teach young folk
that one can't reduce the good life to the shape of a car or
the size of a house. Conscious rappers often spread that
message in creative fashion.

Gibson: Please talk about the impact of crack on hip hop
culture, especially on gangsta rap, which flourished on
the West Coast as an alternative to the conscious rap of
primarily East Coast artists.

Dyson: Well, crack played a big role in hip hop, but even more broadly in black culture in the 1980s, especially out west. This was poignantly portrayed in Gary Webb's three-part series in the *San Jose Mercury*, entitled "Dark Alliance" (which is also the title of a book Webb later wrote on the subject). Webb contended that forces associated with the Contras—or Nicaraguan rebels—were funneling thousands of tons of cocaine into the United States during the 1980s to generate profits for their counterrevolution in Nicaragua. What was especially criminal was how the CIA turned a blind eye (and at other times explicitly aided them, although they were supposed to prevent the infusion of illegal drugs into the United States) as the Contras were flooding poor black communities in Los Angeles and the Bay Area with cocaine, fueling a crack epidemic that devastated thousands of poor blacks and Latinos. So in a sense, elements of our government under Ronald Reagan facilitated the outright destruction of vast reaches of poor black and brown neighborhoods on the West Coast.

All of this nefarious, illegal governmental activity—which essentially bartered black and brown children's lives so that Reagan's allies could support an immoral assault on a foreign power—helped spawn what Mike Davis called the "political economy of crack," or the production, distribution, marketing, and retailing of crack cocaine as a flourishing underground business in poor black America. With the rise of crack, poor black and Latino communities were besieged by drug gangs and increased crime, as well as police surveillance and crackdowns. Besides the fact that poor black and brown communities were flooded with a cheap but lethally addictive form of cocaine, there was the attendant problem of the easy access to automatic weapons. Thus the crack epidemic fostered the rise of violent figures that colonized black urban social space and brought considerable existential terror and domestic trauma in their wake. It also made poor black folk slaves to high-risk diversionary pleasure as a means of psychic survival, discouraging them from directly confronting the social dislocation, the lethargy, and the listlessness that the crack epidemic exacerbated.

The political economy of crack precipitated the rise of gangsta rap on the West Coast. At its beginning, some gangsta rappers were just as eager to narrate the immoral consequences of state-sponsored domestic terror—through police brutality and racial profiling—as they were to glorify guns and gangs. On the East Coast, the Stop the Violence Movement, spearheaded by KRS-ONE, grew out of the desire of several hip hop artists—including Public Enemy, Heavy D, MC Lyte, D-Nice, Kool Moe Dee, and Doug E. Fresh—to challenge the economic and social suffering of poor black communities and force hip hop artists to wrestle with the effects of lending glamour to carnage and mayhem.

As rapper Kool Moe Dee argued in 1989 on "Self-Destruction," the theme song for the Stop the Violence movement, "I never ever ran from the Ku Klux Klan / and I shouldn't have to run from a black man." The Stop the Violence Movement was a conscientious attempt by rappers to interrupt the cycle of black-on-black crime, and to name it as a pathology that should be resisted— not glorified, edified, elevated, or celebrated. That was perhaps the last great hurrah for conscious rap before the full upswing of gangsta rap in the late 1980s and early 1990s.

Gibson: Finally, can you briefly comment on how politics is larger than hip hop culture, even though hip hop can be a vehicle for useful politics?

Dyson: Hip hop can be a critical means to develop and disseminate political consciousness, but the struggle for self-determination, as well as the struggle for human decency and agency, is deeper than any art form. The same struggle has occurred, in varying degrees and certainly with different results, in jazz, blues, gospel, R&B, and most black musical expressions. Hip hop culture has no copyright on political strategies for mobilizing people to protect themselves in a democracy.

But it's important to understand what a critical role hip hop can play in trying to forge political consciousness in young folk. Groups like The Roots, Black Star, De La Soul, and rappers like Ice Cube, J-Live, Gang Starr, Immortal Technique, Slick Rick, and Ras Kass have made politically charged statements on their albums. But politics bleeds beyond narrow definitions of formal utterance, and thus when rappers argue over scarce resources for their poor brothers and sisters, and question why poor black folk don't share in the economic and social bounty of mainstream America, they are also behaving politically.

At their best, hip hoppers have the potential to raise people's awareness. And I think hip hop, if it will challenge and renew itself in the cycles of history and social struggle, can continue to play a vital role in inspiring young folk to become politically astute human beings and citizens. At its best, hip hop can challenge young folk to fight for what they believe in. And it's important for young folk to understand that unless they contribute to their own freedom and self-determination, that freedom and self-determination will mean little. As Frederick Douglass famously argued, "If there is no struggle, there is no progress. Those who profess to favor freedom, and yet depreciate agitation, are men who want crops without plowing up the ground. They want rain without thunder and lightning. They want the ocean without the awful roar of its many waters . . . Power concedes nothing without a demand. It never did and it never will."

But that's not all he said, and people usually fail to quote the rest of Douglass when they cite his familiar words. "Find out just what a people will submit to, and you have found out the exact amount of injustice and wrong which will be imposed upon them; and these will continue till they are resisted with either words or blows, or with both. The limits of tyrants are prescribed by the endurance of those whom they oppress. Men may not get all they pay for in this world; but they must pay for all they get. If we ever get free from all the oppressions and wrongs heaped upon us, we must pay for their removal. We must do this by labor, by suffering, by sacrifice, and, if needs be, by our lives, and the lives of others." That's a healthy reminder for hip hoppers, who must understand that the battles they fight are both more ancient and much larger than hip hop. Yet hip hoppers can find noble cause in preserving the quest for freedom by extending its reach in their lyrical and aesthetic visions.

Killer Mike don't give a damn if it's me you ain't likin' /
The last great debate I had was with Michael Eric Dyson.

—*Killer Mike, "That's Life"*

TRACK 4.

"COVER YOUR EYES AS I DESCRIBE A SCENE SO VIOLENT"

CREDITS

Guest Artist: Byron Hurt

Label: God Bless the Child Productions

Studio Location: Philadelphia

Year Recorded: 2005

Samples: Spelman College Sisters * Elizabeth Spellman * Nelly * Frank Sinatra * The Hebrew Bible (Genesis) * Notorious B.I.G. * Colin Powell * Beverly Guy-Sheftall

Shout Outs: Iconography of Guns * Post-Industrial Urban Space * Sports and Violence * American Military * Republican Party * Black and Latino Machismo * Nelly's "Tip Drill" Video * Anita Hill/Clarence Thomas Controversy * Heterosexism * Homophobia * Homoeroticism * Male Supremacy * Feminism * Visual Injustice * Gendersaurs

Head Nods: Nelly * Notorious B.I.G.

TRACK 4.

"COVER YOUR EYES AS I DESCRIBE A SCENE SO VIOLENT"

Violence, Machismo, Sexism, and Homophobia

Byron Hurt: Hip hop is suffused with violence. One of the recurrent themes that I hear in rap artists' freestyles and in their emcee battles is talk about guns, including GATs, AK-11s, and other weapons. Can you explain that?

Michael Eric Dyson: There's a preoccupation with the gun because the gun is a central part of the iconography of the ghetto. Too many young black and brown men view their sense of strength, and industry, and machismo, and manhood through the lens—and sometimes literally through the scope—of a gun. And what you hear a lot in the lyrics of gangster and hardcore rappers are descriptions of the physical effects of gun violence on the larger community—from the viewpoint of the perpetrators and the victims. The gun is at once the merchandise of manhood and the means of its destruction. The gun is the most lethal means of undermining the masculine stability that many rappers desperately seek.

The gun is a staple of the postindustrial urban setting where young black and brown men contest one another over smaller and smaller living and recreational spaces. The forces of gentrification and decreased availability of affordable housing in the inner city spur rising tensions because of shrunken physical and domestic space. So the gun becomes the violent means by which space is divided and status is assigned. The ghetto teems with arguments made through the barrel of a gun. This homeboy's getting shot at for dancing with the wrong girl at a party; that homeboy's trying to shoot somebody because he feels disrespected on the school playground; another homeboy's shooting back at somebody shooting at him. So the gun becomes the outlet for the aggression and the rage that young black and brown men feel.

We live in a culture where the obsession with the gun is painfully conspicuous, from its ubiquity in Hollywood action films to the ad campaigns for the National Rifle

Association (NRA). No other industrialized nation is so consumed by the gun as the symbol of freedom, which, as it turns out, is the very thing that can lead to bondage to death and destruction. The gun can be the implement of the barbarity of our so-called civilized society. It is the very instrument that's taken up in the fight over the Second Amendment by the NRA and other citizens who believe that their right to own weapons and to possess arms is *the* extension of American freedom.

Hurt: How can you tie notions of black male violence to violent masculinity in American culture more broadly? Please also talk about how hypermasculinity can be seen in other cultural institutions in America—sports culture, military culture, and even presidential politics.

Dyson: Well, simply said, violent masculinity is at the heart of the American identity. The preoccupation with Jesse James, the outlaw, the rebel, the social outcast— much of that is associated in the collective imagination of the nation with the expansion of the frontier in the modern West. Violent masculinity is also tied up with the ability to defend American property from "illegitimate" stakeholders—above all Native Americans, although they were here first and we ripped off their land through a process of genocide that is utterly underappreciated to this day. Violent masculinity is central to notions of American democracy and cultural self-expression.

In fact national self-expression and violent masculinity are virtually concomitant; they came about at the same time, and they often mean the same thing. In the history of the American social imagination the violent male, using the gun to defend his kith and kin, becomes a symbol of virtuous and redemptive manhood. Some young hip hop artists zero in on the use of the gun as the paraphernalia of *American* masculinity, as the symbol of real manhood. Hip hop's hypermasculine pose reflects a broader American trait.

There are so many segments of American society where violence is linked to manhood, from video games to sports like football, hockey, and boxing. Take football, for instance. The guy who delivers the hardest hit while tackling an opponent is most widely celebrated. (Those of us old enough to remember can hardly forget how in a 1978 preseason game, Oakland Raiders football player Jack Tatum, a safety, delivered a vicious blow and broke the neck of New England Patriots wide receiver Darryl Stingley—rendering him a quadriplegic—with no apology, contending at the time that an apology would be an untruthful admission that the hit was dirty.) Sure, there's a cerebral side to sports as well. But it can hardly be denied that sports provide vicarious outlets for millions of fans with a visceral and aggressive payoff.

The stakes of hypermasculinity—or the exaggeration of the posture of manhood and the aggression associated with male identity—are dug deep in our collective psyches. Even in sacred circles aggressive forms of militarism are masked in religious metaphors: God seeks to punish those who disagree with America, and God seeks to put down nations that refuse to obey God. Of course, obeying God and agreeing with America are often conflated in the basest version of our civil theology. This can be clearly seen in religious figures like staunch fundamentalist Jerry Falwell and sophisticated conservative evangelical Ralph Reed.

The American military, of course, makes heroes of those with a command personality and a gung-ho mentality. War is the tragic symbol of the contagious chaos of hypermasculinity, and the leaders of war are the military men we most admire, whether we're speaking of Dwight Eisenhower, Colin Powell, or Norman Schwarzkopf. One of the most potent expressions of hypermasculinity in recent times is the so-called Powell doctrine, epitomized when Colin Powell, in responding to a question about his strategy in combating the Iraqi army in the Persian Gulf War of 1991, said, "First we're going to cut it off, then we're going to kill it." Damn, it just don't get no more violently masculine than that! That kind of testosterone politics brims in masculine quarters of the culture.

And when it comes to politics, especially during a time of national crisis, it's the guy who's willing to deny the need for dissent and debate in order to defend American exploits at all costs who's deemed a "real patriot" and "real man." And make no mistake: the two are joined at the ideological hip. The Republican party often conflates being a hawk with being able to handle national security. War detractors are painted as insufferably weak. Even in colleges and universities, this hyperaggressive masculine image of the professor who refuses to tote the politically correct line prevails in conservative academic quarters, where it's a badge of pride not to embrace multiculturalism in the curriculum. Clearly, hypermasculine images are influential in sports, in the military, in religion, and even in the academy.

Hurt: But isn't that a narrow view of masculinity, especially if we want to remove destructive images of manhood and embrace healthy alternatives?

Dyson: It is a very limiting perspective to see manhood as the ability to impose harm or do violence against another human being, even in retribution against some perceived or real offense. That view of masculinity is truncated and, I would argue, inauthentic. Authentic masculinity is about wisely defining strength and accepting vulnerability. Moreover, American conceptions of masculinity typically fail to acknowledge the virtue in consensus, cooperation, negotiation, and compromise—except in negative enterprises and problematic functions like corporate malfeasance.

When we speak about hypermasculinity, we're speaking about the Frank Sinatratization of American political discourse: "I did it my way." Seeking compromise, looking for consensus, building a healthy coalition—this is not the natural inclination of hyperaggressive males. Such a view of manhood prevents us from reaching out to other nations and seeking agreement and peaceful resolution. Instead we drop bombs on Iraq, warring with a nation that we falsely argued had weapons of mass destruction, and which, contrary to initial claims by some conservatives, had nothing to do with the terrorist attacks of 9/11. We refuse to see how we've precipitated violent responses to our wantonly destructive ways as a nation. We refuse to say to ourselves, "Perhaps our perverted and distorted conception of strength and masculinity has led to some devastating results and has limited the political options we're able to pursue."

Even when we pull back from foreign affairs to focus on domestic issues, our hyperaggressive vision of masculinity is problematic. For instance, patriarchy is the belief that heterosexual white men's lives are normal and any identity that falls outside of such a view is abnormal. Perhaps if we got rid of narrow, rigid quests for manhood in favor of more nuanced conceptions of masculinity, men wouldn't die as much from heart attacks and strokes. We might express ourselves in nonviolent ways and transmit to our boys a more noble and humane vision of manhood. This stuff in the men's movement—about thumping one's chest, going into the woods and beating on drums and giving voice to one's primal scream of masculinity—sometimes works against successful social negotiation in a civil space. That's especially true in the urban situation where testosterone-fueled conflicts often lead to harmful consequences for young men.

Hurt: Could you talk more about what the negative consequences are for black and Latino men, especially in the hip hop generation?

Dyson: Society is teaching many young men and women to believe that the only way to be an authentic man is to dominate a woman. To make matters worse, many young men see women almost exclusively in sexual terms. Violence is also highly glossed and eroticized in hip hop videos and rap lyrics where the appeal of aggression is intensified by the promise of sexualized release. I think real-life relations between young men and women are often trapped in fictional narratives of masculine dominance that hamper the growth of alternative models of healthy male-female relationships.

The moral outrage and feminist ire sparked by Nelly's "Tip Drill" video uncovered a powerful example of such a narrative. I suppose "tip drill" suggests either a female with a nice body but an unattractive face, or a male with a lot of money but an unattractive face. (It also refers to a basketball drill where each player tips the ball off the backboard.) The term also suggests an orgy, or a "train," where several men have sex with a single female. In the video, a young man swipes a credit card through a young woman's gluteus maximus.

Well, I'm hard-pressed to tell the difference between Nelly's video and the time two hundred years ago when black women and men were looked at for their gluteus maximus, for their latissimus dorsi, for their pectoralis major, for their testicles, to see if they were durable enough to procreate in order to extend slavery. Isolating body parts like that represents a sexualized fetish tied to the racial subjugation of black bodies by white suprema- cists. Such a state of affairs reinforces the vulgar status of black humanity, even when it has comic overtones like the troubling image struck in the Nelly video.

You'd think black folk would appreciate the fact that since black bodies were once sold on the auction block, you don't want to perpetuate the sort of visual injustice against women that occurs in the Nelly video. But there's a huge disconnection between older and younger black people that fuels the amnesia that such visual injustice feeds on. Of course, cultural amnesia isn't peculiar to black youth culture; it's really at the heart of American society. We barely remember stuff thirty years ago; God knows we don't remember events from fifty and sixty years ago; and forget history from 150 years ago. So it's very difficult to transmit these values in such cultural and historical circumstances.

In the aftermath of the controversy, the sisters at Spel- man College rightfully opposed Nelly's coming to their

campus, even to raise awareness about bone marrow do-
nation in black communities, unless he was also willing
to sit down and discuss the demeaning messages of his
"Tip Drill" video. Nelly's insulting video was the last
straw for the Spelman women. They had had enough of
the sexist sentiments and patriarchal posturing of young
men who sanctify their bigotry by suggesting it's a natural
male reflex. In the end, Nelly canceled his campus visit
rather than have an open conversation about sexism and
misogyny in hip hop.

I applaud the women of Spelman for their courage.
But the challenge to the sisters of Spelman is to apply
this same moral standard to the clergymen and other
civic and business leaders who are invited to their campus, who hold equally heinous views about women, if not
as obviously virulent as those expressed in hip hop. But
the problematic views of clergy who preach the biblical
basis for female subordination to men, and the harmful
gender views of civic and business leaders, are less likely
to be scrutinized as sexist rap lyrics are. The women of
Spelman must ask themselves if they are willing to be
equally vigilant about decrying the sexism of an upstand-
ing minister or educator as they are a well-known rapper.

Hurt: How do you respond to people who say that the
women at Spelman were being contradictory and hypo-
critical?

Dyson: When the Spelman women took their stand against Nelly, some folk thought it was arbitrary because Nelly is hardly the most sexist or misogynistic rapper one might go after. But one can never predict what controversy will become socially opportunistic and what event will spark outrage or galvanize a community. Nelly's "Tip Drill" visually conjured all the ugly signifiers of black sexism that can be traced back to slavery's crude conception of the black female body. "Tip Drill" created a powerful groundswell of critique and debate. In fact the Spelman sisters' intervention should be applauded and repeated. I don't find them hypocrites at all. I think they acted on what they believed in a given period of time in response to a specific event that inspired their protest. They finally got to the point where the weight of insult on their collective psyches was so crushing that it demanded an immediate response.

In a sense, the Nelly video flap was like the O.J. Simpson case. There were all sorts of arguments about race and the criminal justice system long before O.J. was accused of murder, but O.J.'s criminal case got that idea across like few other events in our nation's history. His case also underscored just how radically different are black and white views on the subject. We couldn't predict that there would be an O.J. Simpson case, or that it would provoke such bitter debate over race in America. Nelly's "Tip Drill" functioned in similar fashion for the debate about sexism in hip hop, although it sparked nothing near the broad cultural conversation that O.J.'s case generated.

There were even some women who criticized the Spelman sisters' decision to make a big deal of the Nelly video and his potential visit to their campus. It just reminds us that we've got to grapple with instances of internalized sexism in women where the ventriloquist magic of patriarchy is occurring—women's lips are moving, but men's voices and beliefs are speaking. I'm not suggesting that *any* female critique of the Spelman sisters was necessarily a patriarchal gesture, but I am saying that a lot of the female criticism of the Spelman sisters suggests how pervasive and irresistible the logic of male supremacy is. Just as some blacks offer the most depressing defense of white supremacy, some women offer tortured defenses of sexism and male supremacy.

Hurt: A lot of people have asked why it took so long for the women of the hip hop generation to take a stand.

Dyson: Well, that's an incredibly shortsighted view of black feminist struggle. Think about the black women associated with African American Women in Defense of Ourselves, the ad hoc collection of women who stood with Anita Hill in her charge that Supreme Court nominee Clarence Thomas had sexually harassed her years before when she worked for him. Thomas had the white male establishment, and a significant portion of the black establishment, on his side. A lot of folk claimed that Hill was self-serving, that her claims were unbelievable because they came so long after the alleged offense, and that she was bringing a black man down and being disloyal to the race.

Some of those same arguments are at work against the Spelman sisters. Some critics claim that it took their generation too long to speak out, and that they were attacking a "good" black man like Nelly who was far from the worst sexist in hip hop. It's clear that some of the same intraracial fault lines that existed with the Thomas/Hill affair are present in the Spelman/Nelly dispute. And it's equally evident that another generation of black women acting in defense of themselves causes problems for patriarchal authority.

The black women who spoke out in defense of Anita Hill were largely established professional black women. They had social savvy and far greater access to media than did the Spelman women. The Spelman women were brilliant, articulate college students confronting huge media forces and the bulwark of black American sexism. The Nelly incident politicized many young black women in the way that the Hill/Thomas affair had done for an earlier generation of black women. We can't forget that black feminist activity has been hampered by black female devotion and loyalty to black men, often at the expense of their own interests and identities.

The Spelman sisters had to grapple with an unfair and absurd question put to activist black women through the ages: "Are you female first or are you black first?" The reality is that black women are black and female simultaneously—and in many cases, poor too. Identity isn't something one can parcel out. As feminist theorist Elizabeth Spellman memorably put it, we must not have an additive vision of identity, where you keep adding elements to increase your minority status—black, female, poor, lesbian, and so on. Still, you can't deny that black women have a lot of complex realities to confront in their bodies. Black women have displayed such extraordinary fidelity to the race that when they finally decide to speak up for themselves, they are viewed as traitors. Black men have often told black women that feminist concerns should only be addressed when the racial question is settled, but we all know that if black women wait that long, justice will never come.

Finally, the question is not what took the Spelman sisters so long to speak up; the question is what took black men so long to realize that we should have spoken out on this issue decades ago. The burden of response shouldn't rest exclusively on black women; the burden of opposing sexism should be shared by our entire community.

And popular culture ain't helping much. I mean, if all you're thinking about as a hormonally driven young male for twenty-four hours a day is the bouncing bosoms and belligerent behinds you see paraded endlessly on music videos, and you're almost exclusively focused on how women can serve your libido, you're not going to have a healthy understanding of women or yourself. If such images are not met with opposing interpretations of black female sexual identity, they can negatively affect the self-understanding and self-image of young black men. They can also have a destructive effect on the erotic and interpersonal relations between young folk.

Another factor that hampers healthy relations is the fact that males are not encouraged to be self-reflective or to take individual and collective self-inventory. To face ourselves is to face the world that men made, and that world doesn't often view women with great respect or appreciation. Young guys don't get a sense that their testosterone plague is somehow related to bigger social and political issues. You can imagine a cat like Nelly saying, "It's just me in the video. I'm just having fun. I'm just blowing off steam. I'm just doing what all guys do."

In this case, the behavior of young black males is isolated from its broader network of social meanings. They don't necessarily get the academic concept of the "social construction of masculinity," which is just a fancy term to say that you ain't born with a sense of what it means to be a man; you're socialized into that. Gender roles are not innate; they're assigned based on what society tells us is good and bad. "You're a woman; you stay home and clean the house and have babies. You're a man; you go out and get a job and support your family." When we begin to challenge those predetermined, heterosexist roles with feminist narratives of gender justice and social equality, we upset the patriarchal applecart. When you've got all that stuff going on around you, it's very difficult for young men to understand that their sexual identities and desires are shaped by the politics and the social struggles of a larger society.

Hurt: How difficult is it for black men to understand that, even though they're the victims of racism, they often perpetuate sexism toward black women?

Dyson: Historically, it has been difficult for black men to understand that although we're victims, we also victimize; that although we're assaulted, we also assault; and that while we're objects of scorn, we also scorn black women as well. As with all groups of oppressed people, it's never a matter of either/or; it's both/and. You can be victimized by white supremacy and patriarchy and at the same time extend black male supremacy. Just because "the white man's foot is on your neck" doesn't mean that your foot can't in turn be on a black female's neck.

We've also got to reckon with how certain forms of male privilege exist precisely because we don't acknowledge them. Male privilege is strongest (so strong that it was one of the first things white men permitted black men to share with them) when we are not forced to interrogate it, when we don't have to ask questions of it.

We insulate ourselves from knowledge of its very existence, and sometimes we do that by seeking refuge in *our* victimization, as if that could prevent us from dealing with how we victimize more vulnerable folk.

In order to understand this, we should think about how race and racism operate for white brothers and sisters. When most of our white brothers and sisters hear the word "race," they think "black" or "brown" or "yellow" or "Native American." They don't think "white," as if white is not one among many other racial and ethnic identities. Men are the same way. When black men hear male supremacy, we often think, "white guys who control the world." We don't think, "Black guys who control our part of the world." You can be oppressed and still be doggin' somebody else who's lower on the totem pole.

In a society dominated by men, women are assigned a lower niche on the societal totem pole. Men often step on the faces of women to climb higher up on the perch of masculine privilege. Our boosted sense of masculinity comes at the expense of women's lives, identities, and bodies.

What's even more telling, but often overlooked, is that black men are also victims of black male supremacy and patriarchy and sexism and misogyny. Those horrible traits actually make *us* worse men. The profound investment in a violent masculinity costs many black men their lives, especially on the streets where codes of respect are maniacally observed and brutally enforced. And closer to home, many black men turn on their loved ones, striking them instead of hitting out at a punishing social order for whom their wives, or girlfriends, or babymamas, or children are the unfortunate proxy. Black men who can't get good jobs often blame their women who are employed. Some brothers blame black women for their success in a zero-sum calculation that suggests women are conspiring against them with white society's approval.

What such brothers fail to understand is how they *and* their women are victims of white male supremacy. Too many brothers fall into the trap of male supremacy by using its logic to explain their absence of payoffs, or rewards, in the patriarchal system. Instead of thinking through the complex dynamics of our vulnerable situation (black women are just as put upon by patriarchy and white supremacy as black men are, even if in different fashion), we become outraged at the women whose love has helped sustain us as men, as a family, and as a race.

Hurt: What about women's complicity in how they are portrayed in rap, especially in videos?

Dyson: Not only are women blamed for the harm that befalls men, but they are blamed for the limitation that male society imposes on them. This is best exemplified by the self-serving justifications commonly offered for the exploitative placement of women in rap videos: "Nobody is making these women appear in the videos; therefore, they must like it and want to do it." But that's like making early black actors the heavies when their only choice in movies was between stereotypical roles. It's not fair to blame them for the white supremacist practices that limited their roles in the first place.

Instead of men saying, "We have limited the roles that black women can play in videos to dime piece, hoochie mama, video vixen, eye candy, arm pleasure, sexy dancer, and more variations of the same," we blame women for accepting the crumbs from our sexist table and trying to eat off of our patriarchal leftovers, as self-destructive and spiritually undernourishing as that may be. We rarely probe the interior of a male-dominated world that forces women into such demeaning choices and roles.

Men just find it easier to blame women for the limited choices *we* leave them with while ignoring the economic and social constraints on young black women who seek a toehold in the world of hip hop culture and rap videos. It's a classic case of blaming the victim, but then there's little difference between what men in hip hop do, and what males in mainstream religion have always done through their theologies and holy texts.

Think back to Genesis 3:12, in the Garden of Eden, where Adam and Eve have disobeyed God and eaten from the forbidden tree only to realize that they're naked. They hide from God when they hear God's voice walking through Eden—I love that metaphor of God's voice walking, quite appropriate for a discussion of the walking voice of hip hop. God calls out to Adam in the Garden of Eden, asking where he is, and Adam finally speaks up, confessing that he's hiding because he's naked. God wonders how he knows he's naked, asking Adam if he's tasted fruit from the tree he wasn't supposed to eat from in the middle of the Garden of Eden. And then Adam blames it all on Eve: "And the man said, the woman whom thou gavest [to be] with me, she gave me of the tree, and I did eat." And of course, Eve blamed the slick serpent for "beguil[ing]" her.

If hip hop has a theology, it's pretty consistent with the biblical justification of male misbehavior by blaming the seducing female. Now that's not to deny that there's female complicity. We have to ask the hard question of why certain women conform to the vicious images of female sexual identity promoted in misogynistic masculinity. Of course, that's not simply a problem that shows up in hip hop; it's a culture-wide phenomenon. When women go to religious institutions where they hear clergy justify their second-class citizenship, they are conforming to the dominant images of a religious culture that aims to subordinate them. But it's easier to jump on hip hop videos than it is to target the sermons of ministers, bishops, imams, and rabbis who reinforce a culture of male privilege and strident patriarchy.

Hurt: Why aren't more men confronting the sexism in hip hop?

Dyson: First, to put it crudely, it's not in their immediate interest to do so. The hip hop industry is built in large measure on the dominant masculine voice, a voice that rarely expresses respect for women as peers—only as mothers. Rappers love their mamas but hate their baby-mamas. Second, it's not as erotically engaging for the men in hip hop to adopt feminist stances, or at the very least, to concede the legitimacy of feminist perspectives. Third, the moment men begin to challenge the retrograde and crude crotch politics of hip hop culture, they feel that they're going to be ostracized.

Well, what hip hop males (and to tell the truth, a lot of older brothers too) don't understand is that one can have really liberating erotic experiences with women as equals. It just never strikes them that they could have beautiful, rapturous, loving, powerful relationships with beautiful, rapturous, loving, powerful, and independent women who don't feel pressure to have sex with men out of a dreadful lack of self-confidence that is encouraged in a brutally sexist culture.

Hurt: A lot of men in hip hop say they want a "good sister" and not a "ho." Of course, that distinction is problematic. What are the limitations of that perspective?

Dyson: Part of the perverse genius of patriarchy is that there's always elbow room for such distinctions and oppositions, like the one between the "good sister" and the "ho." But it's a tricky, loaded juxtaposition indeed. In the parlance, a "good sister" is someone who stays away from "bad boys," who doesn't give sex easily, who keeps herself clear of the troubled circles that men in hip hop frequent. A "ho" is a loose woman who gives sex easily, who drinks and smokes and is found in the company of males in hip hop.

What's interesting about such an ethical division between women is that the men in hip hop have much more experience with the ho than they do the good sister. The good sister they claim to adore—well, they don't spend that much time with her. In part, that's because the good sister, in their minds, is not the one most likely to concede to their erotic advances or otherwise behave as the men do. The ho, ironically enough, even as she is castigated, is granted a strange equality of ends with the males in hip hop: they both want the same thing, at least when it comes to sex, drugs, and music, even if they seek it for different ends—the men to flex their muscles of manhood, the women to enhance their access to male circles of power, privilege, and pleasure.

But isn't it interesting that males in hip hop have much more ethnographical data on the ho than on the good sister? They spend more time pursuing, pleasing, and "playing" the ho than the good sister, even though they often put the latter on a social pedestal. But the notion of placing women on a pedestal of respect is a severely limiting gesture. Respect can reinforce the "proper" role of women, which often means denying them the sexual pleasures, social standing, cultural perks, and erotic freedom that men routinely enjoy. Respect can be an iron fist in a velvet glove. Patriarchal notions of respect—such as keeping women at home away from the fray of professional spheres—often mock true independence of thought and behavior for women.

This understanding of respect means that a good sister must do more than not act like a ho to win male approval. For instance, a woman who shows no ho tendencies but challenges male conceptions of power and authority, or makes more money than her man and doesn't pretend that she doesn't, is a problem to her man as well. In many cases, her independent, challenging behavior is read as disrespectful. Upon closer inspection, the good sister/ho opposition doesn't hold up in defining the critical difference between the desirable/undesirable woman, because other elements intrude.

Too often, putting a woman on a pedestal of respect is the attempt to control her by softer, more subtle means. And the moment a woman steps off that pedestal—even if she's otherwise viewed as respectable—she's a problem. In the crude language of patriarchal disdain, she's a "bitch," the equally derided, often more powerful ideological twin of the "ho." Women who confront and vacate the pedestals of patriarchal respectability are viewed as bitches or hoes.

Hurt: You hear male rap artists constantly use "bitch" or "ho" to feminize other men. What does that reveal about black masculinity?

Dyson: The greatest insult from one man to another in hip hop (and beyond) is to imply that he's less than a man by calling him a derogatory term usually reserved for women or gay men: "bitch," "ho," "punk," "fag." It's an act of enhanced degradation because injury is added to insult with the double negative of being dissed to begin with and then being assigned a gender or sexual orientation epithet to boot. These epithets place a male lower on the totem pole of masculine identity by classifying him with the already degraded female or gay male.

In regard to women, look how deadly such an identification is, being made the ultimate equivalent of a despised male. This underscores another harmful use of "bitch" by men: it is what philosophers might call a "multievidential" term. It fits a lot of circumstances and can be used in multiple ways to either affirm or negate a specific identity or instance. It can be used to suggest good and bad, sometimes at the same time, and in the case of hip hop, sometimes in the same lyric. When the late Notorious B.I.G. created the song "Me and My Bitch," he didn't mean anything negative by the use of the term. He was celebrating his female companion. Others use the term regularly to suggest both meanings—problematic female or loving female companion—or women in general.

In fact, for many in hip hop, saying "bitch" is natural, like saying "woman."

Of course, in hip hop as in the larger society you pick on the most vulnerable when you want to insult somebody. In our society, that's women, gays, and lesbians. Children are vulnerable too, but they're not usually attacked in hip hop circles.

More specifically, the accepted and misguided notions of maleness in society dictate which types of homosexuality are more tolerable. What's quite interesting, perhaps even paradoxical, is that hip hop in this regard reflects the values of mainstream conservative culture when it comes to the victimization of women, gays, lesbians, bisexuals, and transgender folk. And not just among white folk either. We're having a huge debate right now in American society about gay and lesbian marriage, and one thing we can depend on is black and brown communities offering extraordinary support to a conservative president and his allies in their assault on the liberties and civil rights of these gay and lesbian people. The president appeals to conservative evangelical beliefs about sexuality and gender, and a narrow, literal reading of the Bible that appeals to a lot of blacks and Latinos. That always trips me out because I wonder how people who were illiterate less than 150 years ago could be biblical literalists!

After all, the same religious folk who historically subscribed to a biblical literalism that castigated black folk and justified our oppression and enslavement now use the same principles of interpretation to justify resistance to gays and lesbians. And many black folk are in league with them. That's just crazy, and I say this as an ordained Baptist preacher rooted deeply in progressive evangelical territory. There is huge support for biblical texts that justify assault on gay and lesbian identity—or, for that matter, on women as first-class citizens. Ironically enough, hip hop, which is equally reviled in conservative circles and in many quarters of established black America, for its allegedly decadent morality, is in full agreement with these regressive viewpoints.

Of course, the sin of hip hop to many who abhor hip hoppers' virulent expression of sexism and misogyny is that they are explicit and vulgar in articulating their beliefs. What is required are the more subtle, sophisticated expressions of misogyny and patriarchy that are not nearly as outwardly venomous as the female antipathy found in hip hop. Hip hop captures the bigotry toward women and gays and lesbians found in the larger society—but on steroids, so to speak. It's the ugly exaggeration of viewpoints that are taken for granted in many conservative circles across the nation.

Of course, all of us have to confront the sexism, misogyny, patriarchy, and homophobia that are so deeply rooted in our culture. I try to embrace and live feminist principles, but I'm constantly at war with the deeply ingrained sexism of the culture that seeps into my brain. The same is true for homophobia. That's the challenge I face: to confront and reject male supremacy and hetero-sexist bigotry even as we together confront and reject them in the broader society.

Hurt: I'm against homophobia, but if I see a gay person kissin' somebody of the same sex on TV, I'm like, "Oh!"

Dyson: But if we, as heterosexual men, see two lesbians kissing each other, not only are we not necessarily turned off, we may even be turned on. Lesbian sexuality can in some cases be tolerated, even encouraged, because it can be subordinated to the heterosexual male erotic econ-omy: two for the price of one. We can swing the women our way to allow us to participate in a ménage à trois! You can imagine a brother saying, "Oh, I don't mind if you get into bed with me with your other girl because she might please us both." So there's room in the heterosex-ual world for situational lesbianism that services the straight male crotch.

Hurt: Talk about the weird tension between homophobia and homoeroticism in hip hop.

Dyson: What's intriguing to me about the tensions and therefore the connections between homophobic and ho-moerotic men is that they both have a stake in the same body. Straight and gay men are equally invested in the same testosterone-soaked athletic contest where men are slapping each other's behinds on the football field or patting each other's booties after making a touchdown. The same straight and gay males go to church and leap to their feet and vigorously ejaculate, "I love him! I love him," speaking about another man—Jesus.

One of the reasons there's so much tension between men who can be virulently homophobic and those who can be vibrantly homoerotic (and make no mistake, they are often the same guys, except one group isn't aware of it) is because they both have investments in the same body. The same actions can count as grandly heterosexual or gleefully homoerotic. Slapping behinds, patting booties, hugging, and hollering about Jesus—all that is multievidential. Those actions count for heterosexuals and homosexuals at the same time, depending on how you interpret them.

To the horror of straight men, they're engaging in a lot of actions that could easily be interpreted as gay. I mean, I often joke with my son, "If you're so interested in protecting yourself from gay men, you're giving somebody an easy shot at your butt with your pants sagging so low and your drawers showing." So even in the most hallowed heterosexual circles, homoerotic bonding occurs on the regular. That's bound to cause a lot of straight guys to worry about their own sexuality, or to ask if what they're doing is pure or is contaminated with homoerotic sentiment. You can see how easily that might lead these straight men to question themselves and then direct enormous fury at gay males and gay culture. It's precisely because the meanings are shared, and the significations slide easily between straight and gay male culture, that there is such huge hatred for homosexuals among heterosexual men.

What's more, the gay male upsets the social order for the straight male. The straight male wants at the male body of his friends and comrades without the attribution of homoerotic union or homosexual desire. Straight males want to celebrate the athletic body, the cultural body, and the religious body without fear of being charged with an erotic or sexual attraction to it. The presence of a gay male throws things off, and therefore the straight male argues for erotic segregation, so that rigid lines can be drawn between the kind of desire the gay male has and the kinds of social and personal interests that animate the heterosexual male. You can understand that there'd be a lot of self-questioning, self-doubting, and questioning and doubting of others as a result of homoerotic desire invading the precincts of straight male desire.

It even invades the religious realm and the church sanctuary, where the tension between heterosexual and homosexual elements is especially pronounced—from the pulpit to the choir stand—and therefore vehemently resisted. You've got "straight" men proclaiming their love for Jesus, even more than their love for parents, partners, or progeny. And even though they consider him God, he's still embodied on earth as a man. So their love for

another man supersedes their love for anything or anybody else. In some readings, that's awfully homoerotic,
maybe even a supernaturally supported homoeroticism.

Homoerotic moments show up in hip hop in at least a
couple of ways. First, when hip hop artists speak about
M.O.B. (money over bitches), they are emphasizing the
crass relation between commerce and misogyny. But
there's another element to M.O.B. as well: placing
"homies" above women, because men make money with
men—or take money from them. In any case, the male
relation becomes a fetish in hip hop circles: hanging with
"my boys," kicking it with "my crew," hustling with "my
mens and them," and dying for "my niggas." There is an
unapologetic intensity of devotion that surely evokes at
some level homoerotic union.

Second, there is great exaggeration or even mythology
about sexual conquests performed in the presence of one
or more participating men. "I hit it, then my boy hit it,"
some young men brag, while others boast of multiple
men having consensual sex with a woman. One assumes
that males expose their sexual organs in such conquests,
especially as they mimic the sexual gestures adapted from
the pornographic tapes that are increasingly popular in
certain hip hop circles. This is surely a heated and heady
moment of homoerotic bonding.

Hurt: Finally, how do you respond to someone like Beverly Guy-Sheftall who says that often the issues that are

prioritized, even in conscious hip hop, are issues that impact black men: racial profiling, the prison-industrial complex, police brutality, and so on. She argues that hip hop rarely deals with gender issues—sexism and misogyny—and never addresses homophobia.

Dyson: Well, there's no question that we've got to teach these young black men to be concerned about issues beyond their own body and bailiwick. But let's be honest: that makes them no different than most men in America. Dr. Guy-Sheftall, whom I admire greatly, is absolutely right. But as I'm sure she'd agree, that point can also be made about most civil rights leaders as well, or most black captains of industry. That point can be made about male television executives in charge of featuring women baring their bosoms and bopping their behinds on music videos all day. So the critique is right on, even though it can't be made exclusively about young black men.

But we've all got to learn as black men—whether in hip hop or business, academe or acting—that sexism and misogyny *are* our issues and *do* affect us as black men, because a world that makes women less than they ought to be, makes us as men less than we ought to be. We are not real men when we deny women their rightful place in our society or attack the networks of formal and informal support they have generated out of necessity. When men in hip hop finally learn that, they will be far ahead of men in other quarters of the culture who may appear to

> Without question, Michael Eric Dyson is among
> the most dynamic teachers that I have ever met.
> He is remarkably well-informed and equally approachable.
> And on top of that, he ain't no square. You gotta love that.
>
> —*Mos Def*

TRACK 5. (THE GENDER REMIX)

"NAPPY-HEAD HO'S, WORSE THAN BITCH NIGGAZ"

CREDITS

Guest Artist: James Peterson

Label: Penn State Abington

Studio Location: Philadelphia, New York City, and Chicago

Year Recorded: 2007

Samples: Don Imus * Richard Rorty * V. S. Naipaul * Spike Lee * Snoop Dogg

Shout Outs: Misogyny * Black Female Sexual Identity * Spike Lee * Rutgers University Women's Basketball Team * Black Hair * Don Imus * Mamas and Babymamas * Media * School Daze * Black Male Accountability * Free Speech * Artistic Responsibility * Senate Hearings on Rap * Generational Conflict * Black Male Elegance * Black Fathers and Daughters * Styles of Black Music * Strippers * Duke Rape Case * Death of Hip Hop

Head Nods: Black Thought * Ja Rule * Nas * Jay-Z * 2Pac * Snoop Dogg * Chuck D * Diddy * Queen Latifah

TRACK 5.
(THE GENDER REMIX)

"NAPPY-HEAD HO'S, WORSE THAN BITCH NIGGAZ"

Don Imus, the Crisis of Patriarchy, and the Death and Rebirth of Hip Hop

James Peterson: Black people, especially black leaders and figures throughout black media, were enraged over Don Imus's egregious comment that the members of the Rutgers University women's basketball team were "nappy-headed ho's." How do you read Imus's comments in light of our charged racial history?

Michael Eric Dyson: We've got to heed the phrase Don Imus used in his defense after the public outcry over his horrible comments: context matters. Imus was referring to how he is a comedic entertainer whose words should be viewed in a humorous vein. There is little evidence, however, that a broadcaster of his weightiness and influence is seen primarily as a comedian. The context that is important for interpreting the Imus controversy is twofold. First, this isn't the first time that Imus, or colleagues on his show, have overstepped the boundaries of ethical sensitivity in speaking crudely of black folk. He referred to respected PBS anchor Gwen Ifill as a "cleaning lady" and called noted sports columnist William Rhoden a "*New York Times* quota hire." Sid Rosenberg was fired from his job supplying sports updates on Imus's show in 2005 for cruel comments about Australian singer Kylie Minogue's breast cancer diagnosis ("She won't look so pretty when she's bald with one titty.") It was also Rosenberg who suggested that Venus and Serena Williams were better suited to appear in *National Geographic* than *Playboy* magazine. Unsurprisingly, Rosenberg was on the phone talking with Imus when he made his fateful comments about the Rutgers players.

Second, we've got to put Imus's words about the Rutgers women's basketball team into cultural context. After saying that he watched the NCAA championship game between Rutgers and the University of Tennessee, Imus said, "That's some rough girls from Rutgers. Man, they got tattoos and . . ." Before he could finish his words, his executive producer Bernard McGuirk chimed in, "Some hard-core ho's." Not wanting to be outdone, Imus retorted, "That's some nappy-headed hoes there. I'm gonna tell you that now, man, that's some woo. And the girls from Tennessee, they all look cute, you know, so, like kinda like I don't know." Although Imus was at a loss for words, McGuirk readily supplied the missing inspiration by drawing on black film history. "A Spike Lee thing," McGuirk said as Imus agreed. "The 'Jigaboos' vs. the 'Wannabes' that movie that he had." Although the movie was cited as *Do the Right Thing*, it was actually *School Daze*. Rosenberg and McGuirk then disparagingly compared the Rutgers players to professional male basketball teams like the Toronto Raptors and the Memphis Grizzlies.

This is disturbing on many levels. Spike Lee satirized the intraracial tensions on a fictional college campus between dark-skinned, community-based, politically oriented, natural-hairstyle-sporting young black women termed the "Jigaboos" versus fair-skinned, contact-lens-wearing, self-absorbed, elitist young women called the "Wannabes." By calling the Tennessee players "cute," it's apparent that Imus was suggesting that the Lady Vols, with several fairer-skinned black players, were the "Wannabes" and the darker Rutgers players were the "Jigaboos." Since American standards of beauty are shaped by the cultural obsession with white ideals and tastes, lighter-skinned black folk have always had a perceived aesthetic leg up on their darker kin.

By referring to the Rutgers players as "nappy-headed ho's," Imus achieved a sinister dual impact: he confirmed brutal stereotypes about black female promiscuity and hypersexuality, and he reinforced the vulnerability black women experience over their hair as a symbol of their aesthetic alienation from norms of white beauty. From the beginning of slavery, black women have been viewed as deviant sexual beings possessed of insatiable carnal urges. Black women were viewed as oversexed because they had to meet the erotic demands of their sexually feared black men. Until the second half of the twentieth century, black women were seen as incapable of being raped; their alleged exceptional sexual capacity meant that no white man would have to take what they would freely offer.

Black women have also endured stigma and withering stares at their resilient coifs. The way many white women effortlessly whip their hair over their shoulders is an erotic gesture that seals their attractiveness and stylistically separates them from many black women who are viewed as unattractive. Hair has long been for black American women a sore spot—often quite literally when you consider the lengths black women go to embrace or conquer their "nappy" hair, whether through relaxers, weaves, or extensions. Black women's hair is among the most vulnerable features of their bodies because it embodies visible differences that are used to distinguish their beauty, or its absence, from that of nonblack women. Black women experience intense anxiety in deciding to either straighten their hair, or to plait, braid, or lock it in dreads. Black people have psychologically absorbed this toxic self-hatred by scorning black women who wear a natural hairstyle. But when black women comb through their contradictions there's usually no mirror in white America to capture their struggles.

Of course, the great irony of Imus's attack is that hardly any of the black women on the Rutgers basketball team had braids, plaits, or natural hairstyles. Most of them had straightened hair that reflects the ideal standard and taste of white beauty. Obviously Imus's bigotry against dark black skin and style overwhelmed his optic nerves and provided a perception that, at least when it involved hair, couldn't even be empirically verified.

Peterson: How has hip hop culture and the language of rap music shaped the commentary on Imus's racist slippage and the societal outcry that led to his dismissal, first from MSNBC, which simulcast his radio show, and a day later, from his main job at CBS radio?

Dyson: Nearly all parties involved in this tragic spectacle —Imus, black and other female leaders, critics and protesters—agree that rap music plays a big role in the degradation of black women. It's been instructive to gauge the response of broad sections of white America to the Imus controversy. Pundits and citizens alike have weighed in on the apparent hypocrisy of black leaders and critics lambasting Imus for his coarse comments on black women while ignoring routine public airing of black misogyny. Imus went as far as to say, "I may be a white man, but I know that . . . young black women all through that society are demeaned and disparaged and disrespected . . . by their own black men and that they are called that name." Imus said that rappers "defame and demean black women" and call them "worse names than I ever did." Hip hop is blamed for the racist assault on young black women by a powerful, arrogant sixty-six-year-old white man who probably couldn't tell you the difference between Black Thought and Ja Rule. It's apparent that Imus and many critics have got the line of detrimental influence backward: it's not that hip hop has helped mainstream the misogyny that its artists *invented*. It's that the ancient vitriol toward women has been amplified in the mouths of some young black males.

Disappointingly, many white pundits and journalists only seem to bring up hip hop's vastly harmful role in spewing venom toward black women when it suits *white* media and political purposes. The tone of the objections follows a familiar pattern, particularly on television: the journalist admits that Imus was wrong; the journalist proceeds to indict him briefly for his faux pas; the journalist often cites the good work Imus did in his career, especially since some of them witnessed it firsthand during appearances on his show; the journalist then suggests that Imus is hardly the worst offender since rappers routinely pelt black women with misogynistic words; and the journalist wants to know what the guest thinks about such hypocrisy, and spends the bulk of time on what must now be done to remedy the problem.

On the surface, that sounds reasonable and fair. But on closer inspection, we may reasonably question the motives at work. If there were genuine concern for the role of rap in ruining young black women's self-esteem, there would have been far greater media coverage of past attempts by black leaders and critics to wrestle with the misogyny of hip hoppers. In 1990, Queen Latifah courageously assailed misogyny by asking in her song "U.N.I.T.Y.," "Who you callin' a bitch?" There was little media fanfare. In 1994, I participated in a Senate hearing before Senator Carol Moseley-Braun and others about the effect of gangsta rap lyrics on black youth, with nowhere near the same media coverage. The same is true for a 2000 Senate hearing in which I participated before Senators John McCain, John Kerry, and Sam Brownback exploring the marketing of violence to children. Liberal political activist C. Delores Tucker and Harlem pastor Rev. Calvin Butts in the early 1990s sought to rid rap music of misogyny. Tucker (who sometimes joined forces with conservative political figure Bill Bennett) went after the corporations that distribute gangsta rap with modest success; Butts eventually drove a steamroller over a pile of tapes and CDs in a symbolic gesture of black outrage against youthful mass-marketed misogyny from the mouths of rap artists. Both received ephemeral press coverage. Various campaigns by Rev. Jesse Jackson and Rev. Al Sharpton opposing violence and misogyny in rap music in the 1990s and into the new millennium have barely been mentioned. The response of some Spelman College women in 2004 to Nelly's "Tip Drill" video drew hardly any notice from the mainstream press. Since 2005, *Essence* magazine has been involved in a project, Take Back the Music, aimed at criticizing, and cleaning up, rap music's gender bashing, but with little press coverage.

The white media have largely ignored black resistance to rap's rhetorical malevolence. In compensation for their ignorance, journalists presiding over the coverage of the Imus controversy often charged their black guests— directly or by implication because of their color—with a troubling complicity in a moral failure that more aptly reveals the ethical blindness and indifference of mainstream media. The alleged failure of black folk to go after our own youth in their assault on our women is not used primarily to strengthen the case of black women, but to enhance Imus's standing (not his stance) as a media creature in league with black offenders who have done far worse. In that strict sense, black women are being pimped again and thus turned into "ho's" by the very media ostensibly committed to their defense. The black female's body is only of value as it serves the interests of white corporate media to pinpoint the true pathology of misogyny as a black moral lapse and not a white moral failure. Black women's bodies are hardly ever the subject of sustained "care" and sympathetic media scrutiny, except when they are a case in point for a mainstream political or moral agenda. This ploy prevents the media from inspecting its hind parts and taking rigorous account of its unseemly role in perpetuating images and stereotypes that degrade and devalue black women.

The self-righteous tone of some journalists also obscures the fact that one explanation for the lack of coverage of black protest against negative images of black females in hip hop has to do with the overwhelming white cast to the media. As I participated in the media scrutiny of the coverage in both print and electronic media, I was struck by the unintended revelation of the proceedings: media remains the domain of the white and wealthy. Black experts were imported from academe, journalism, and entertainment to feed the ravenous appetite of the twenty-four-hour news beast of cable television. Their presence gave the lie to claims during less intense periods of news coverage that few black experts could be found to fill guest lists. The impressive array of black pundits, critics, talking heads, leaders, businesspeople, and the like proved that there is a wealth of wisdom and insight into black life and occasionally, just as much tomfoolery, posturing, and inane commentary as occurs in white circles. Why such folk are not routinely brought onto network and cable television to offer their views cannot be chalked up to mystery, but rather to the failure of behind-the-scenes decision makers to call on such talent, and not for discussions of race alone.

Although the black punditocracy offered varying analyses about the relative impact of rap music and videos on the negative portrayal of black females, most agreed that the genre must be indicted for its lethal gender views. While hip hop certainly must be held accountable for its gleeful circulation of hateful views of black females, a white public figure like Imus, who has far more power and legitimacy than most rappers, must not be allowed to escape responsibility for his grievous error by pointing the finger at black pop music. Before his firing from MSNBC and CBS, Don Imus held forth as an arbiter of public opinion who hosted political powerhouses and pop stars, as well as prominent members of mainstream media. Snoop Dogg's misogyny *is* horrible. His MTV-aired defense of rappers calling "hood" women "ho's" as qualitatively different than Imus calling female college students "ho's" is nonsensical, vulgar, and classist, and should be opposed with just as much vigor as Imus's comments. Snoop Dogg doesn't host a radio show to spew hatred over public airwaves with the imprimatur of CBS or MSNBC. An offensive hip hop artist or rap song is not the cultural equivalent of a talk show host. An artist possesses a different set of liberties, expectations, and conventions than a host who operates under a specific set of rules and limitations.

Free speech for artists, where you can curse on a record or at a comedy concert, differs from the restrictions imposed on conversation across public airwaves. That's another ballgame altogether; Imus has a gravitas that rappers don't begin to approach. It is a red herring to suggest hip hop's undeniable virulence toward black females as a justification for the bleak antipathy toward black women that grips mainstream American culture. White culture venomously attacked black women long before the birth of hip hop, which helps explain Imus's beliefs. It is entirely tragic that hip hop has done more than its share to disseminate such madness toward black females. In fact, hip hop has made the assault on black women stylish and perhaps more acceptable by supplying linguistic updates (like the word "ho") to deeply entrenched bigotry. Hip hop has unquestionably helped desensitize our culture to the systematic attack on black females' lives.

Beyond hip hop, a disturbing trend has gripped black America: young black males who love their mamas but loathe their "babymamas." Of course past generations of black males lauded their mothers while enduring tensions with their girlfriends and wives. It's natural that occasionally men verbally spar with the women they love, even their mothers. But it is the public character of these bitter disputes that has made them especially chilling among black males. One of the reasons black males are vocal about conflicts with the mother of their children is that they're often young when fatherhood comes calling. Teen fathers who are barely grown themselves may lack the maturity to handle their beefs in private. As a former teen father with a turbulent first marriage, a union that was forged after my girlfriend became pregnant, I know firsthand how arguments between young parents can slip easily into public view. Fortunately, I had a caring father and a pastor who counseled me not to resolve domestic differences on the sidewalk.

Today many young black males face such challenges without fathers or mentors who model healthy behavior. This increases the likelihood that black males will repeat destructive cycles in relating to the mother of their children. It is a good idea to offer parenting classes to young black folk to help them cope with the distress that all couples confront. But there are circumstances that worsen the plight of young fathers and mothers, including the impermanence of their relationships, poor choices in partners, inferior education, poverty, and a crumbling floor of economic and employment opportunity. No wonder young black parents turn on each other. But the way young black males lash out at young mothers is all the more depressing.

The assault on young black mothers is fueled by the sexism and misogyny that riddle mainstream and minority culture. It is an ancient practice for men to blame women for their ills, and many men hold to a double standard when it comes to nurturing, loving, and protecting children. This hypocrisy blares when black comedians note how young black mothers shirk their responsibility to their children when they party during the week, leaving their kids at home alone or with questionable caretakers. But these comedians offer little criticism of the males who either abandon or show little regard for their brood.

Such moral contradictions existed long before rap music. Still, it must be admitted that hip hop culture has offered a bruising reverberation of such painful domestic tendencies. There is a great deal of mother love among hip hop artists. In "Dear Mama," Tupac Shakur summarized his mother's flaws and virtues in a single phrase: "And even as a crack fiend mama / You always was a black queen mama." And recently, Jay-Z celebrated his mother by asking the world to offer a "toast to the most beautiful girl in the world / My inspiration, thanks for your information." But for every paean to motherhood, there seem to be ten songs that insult, dismiss, harangue, berate, and degrade young black women who are lovers and mothers. The artists who draw such demeaning portraits of young women often ignore the contradiction that snares them: praising their mamas, slamming their babymamas. The relentless rhetorical attack on young black mothers in hip hop spreads vicious myths and stereotypes about young black mothers. It also reinforces their social fragility.

We need mature young black males to speak up about the accountability of young black men to their families. We also need more critics of the social obstacles that keep young black males from acting responsibly toward the mothers of their children. And we certainly need healthier visions of young black mothers in black popular culture. Jay-Z nods toward such a stance in his song "Lost Ones." Here the rapper eloquently mourns the failure of a relationship by expressing qualities his peers have been slow to embrace: tenderness toward the woman he loved, empathy for her struggles, and a mature self-critique that spares him a bitter view of their time together. Older blacks can encourage an uplifting view of black mothers by supporting and mentoring younger blacks in their relationships. We can also fight sexism wherever we find it, including in our mosques, temples, and sanctuaries, and in our living rooms too. We must convince young black males to treat their babymamas with as much love and respect as they give their mamas.

Peterson: Do you think if older black men mentored younger black males there would be fewer public expressions of misogyny that have become depressingly routine? Of course, we'd have to resolve the huge generational tensions that have plagued the relations between older and younger black males.

Dyson: I think you're right. The generational conflict between black males has turned ugly. Older black men routinely put young black males down for their clothes, their music, and their corrupt values. Younger black men protest that their elders are stuck in the past and lack appreciation for their contributions and struggles. The truth is that older and younger black men have a lot to gain from each other. At their best, older black men possess a remarkable sense of elegance. Black male elegance often consisted of more than stylish dress. In earlier times, it was a protest as well against disparaging views of black culture by ignorant or bigoted whites. If blacks were viewed as crude and barbaric, their dress would testify to their dignity and resilience. Black men who were forced to do menial labor during the week donned suits and ties on the weekend to play and pray. Clubs were full of brothers who took enormous pride in fine and flamboyant get-ups. Churches were jammed with black men giving honor to God in well-tailored jackets, pressed pants, and starched shirts.

That sense of style has carried over into the next generation, often without recognition. But something else has happened: poor black males who lack social support, and sometimes care at home, have covered up in clothes more suited to prison than the sanctuary or the boardroom. Sagging pants and oversize shirts are at once the sign of black youth's alienation from their elders, an embrace of street values, a stop along the path to adulthood, and an ingenious way for a few of them to turn urban style into millions of dollars. Jay-Z now wears expensive tailor-made suits because he spoke the verse of alienated youth as a former street hustler who "changed clothes" as he matured. Besides that, thousands of black youth reared on hip hop enjoy well-being in corporate America. Sure, they dress for success, but that's because street style fueled an interest in black culture that has created opportunity for lawyers, entrepreneurs, and other professionals eating from hip hop's table. It's also proof that old-style elegance and new-style dress, and the black men who choose either, have been of great mutual benefit.

Of course, older black men dig their blues and jazz, their gospel and their soul music—but so do a lot of younger black men who hunger for real music that's not overproduced or technologically manipulated. A lot of younger black men love John Coltrane and Miles Davis, groove with Marvin Gaye, and still have a thing for Aretha Franklin. And it's not lost on some old heads how the most conscientious rappers, including 2Pac, Chuck D, and Nas, join politics and partying. Neither should it be lost on us how we make demands of hip hoppers that we rarely make of other artists. Did anyone demand that George Clinton make politically astute music? Does anyone complain that Brian McKnight hasn't sung redemptive hymns to spark or accompany social protest? Does anyone care that Luther Vandross sang beautiful ballads while neglecting race relations or ecology? The argument in defense of artists who don't rap for a living is that at least they don't degrade women or flaunt social pathology in their art.

Misogyny and moral mayhem are surely reason for concern, although that hasn't stopped folk from going to church, attending college, or working in the corporate world. All of these arenas feature these harmful traits in abundance. Admittedly, they're smoothed over and made far more subtle. But that may be the ultimate sin of younger black men in the eyes of their elders: they just can't seem to finesse the ugliness and prefer to let it all hang out. For older black men, that was a taboo. It's one thing to *be* a misogynist; it's another thing to celebrate it before the world. The older guys have a point: if you parade your vicious thoughts, you often fail to challenge or contain such beliefs. But the younger guys have a point too: if you keep such views private, you're seduced into a false sense of moral superiority over those who struggle openly with their flaws.

I think there's a challenge that black leaders and other critics of rap music must take up: to resist the virus of misogyny, sexism, patriarchy, and femiphobia in mainstream black institutions as well as in hip hop culture. For instance, black women make up nearly 80 percent of many black churches, pay their tithes, and offer moral and spiritual support; yet they can't officially lead the institution they numerically dominate because of continuing sexist and patriarchal beliefs. Those black women are the victims of ecclesiastical apartheid. In the most base sense imaginable their money is used to subsidize their oppression, transforming them into ecclesiastical hoes. Now that's something that leaders like Jesse Jackson and Al Sharpton and the rest of us may take up with as much vigor as we do the fight against misogyny in hip hop. One variety of sexism is more visible, and the other strain more subtle, but the same message of second-class citizenship for black females is being communicated.

Peterson: In the midst of the Imus affair, three members of the Duke men's lacrosse team had all criminal charges against them dismissed in an infamous case where they were charged, among other things, with rape of a young black female student who also was a stripper. Another hip hop generation black woman's reputation and life have been irrevocably altered in the public sphere. Philosophically speaking, who does this young black woman's body belong to now—to her, to the media, to the black community, to her critics and disbelievers? In what ways are these real-life narratives in dialogue with, or influenced by, the misogynistic discourses in the broader culture and in rap music?

Dyson: Well, you've got to remember that, as a black woman, symbolically speaking, her body was never really hers to begin with. Sure, she may have had it for the twenty-seven years she's been on earth. But her body, like all black women's bodies, never really belonged to her. Or maybe it never belonged *just* to her. Her body belongs to a nation that sold black bodies like cattle. It belongs to a court that said that black folk had no rights that white folk were bound to respect. It belongs to a religion that said that God saved African savages from their heathen homeland. It belongs to a region of citizens that went to war against their kin rather than give up the right to breed black bodies and keep them in bondage.

But her body also belongs to higher powers. It is on loan from the God who decided to give her life. At least that's what she's probably been told from the time she was a little girl. Back then theology made little sense except when there were stern reminders that "your body is a temple of the Holy Spirit." If her family didn't tell her, the church did, even if she didn't sit in its pews. The black church shows up whenever black folk say that God told them to love you, or help you, or instruct you, or uplift you. It also shows up when some of them tell you that you're going to hell because you don't believe the way they believe. Or because you behave the way they *used* to behave before Jesus saved them from the lake of fire. It shows up when sisters who mean no harm tell you to watch how you prance and switch. After all, if your body sways the wrong way, it might even sway holy men to forget that your body belongs to God. Next thing you know they'll be borrowing his temple for a night and telling you that joy isn't the only thing that comes in the morning.

Her body also belongs to every music video that pictures her as a hoochie, or trick, or gold digger, or chicken head, or skeezer, or hoodrat, or slut. Her body belongs to the slow-motion frames that capture her breasts jiggling, her hips gyrating, her behind protruding, and her torso writhing in sensual conniptions. She belongs to every lyric that tags her "bitch" or "ho." She also belongs to every voyeur who pounds his flesh in the dark to splash on her ebony eroticism. She belongs to every fantasy of furious sex conjured by the pulsating rhythms of pelvic thrusts. She belongs to every would-be stud that peels off his roll of dollar bills to stuff into her moving g-string.

She belongs to every woman who, in order to feed her children and put herself through school, has to dance for a living, either by twirling around a pole in a club or spiraling up corporate stairs to a glass ceiling. She belongs to every woman who has had to hear that if she hadn't been acting so sexy she wouldn't have been raped. But she belongs, even more, to black women. She belongs to that little black girl who was molested by her uncle and then intimidated into silence. She belongs to that black girl with budding breasts who was seduced by a man claiming to be her "play father." She belongs to that teenage black girl who was sexually abused by her mother's boyfriend, and then thrown out of the house when her mother desperately needed to believe her lover more than her daughter.

She belongs to the black girl who committed suicide with her mother when they discovered they were both sleeping with the same married minister. She belongs to the black girl who was murdered by her mother's live-in companion because she might tell how he had taken her virginity when she was eleven. She belongs to the college student who was date-raped and hushed into shameful self-denial by repeating inside her brain all the reasons why she wasn't really raped. She belongs to those other young women who have to escort men in order to usher kids into adulthood. She belongs to those young ladies who are reprimanded by their elders with harsh judgment. "If you hadn't been acting like a loose woman in an immoral profession, you wouldn't have been abused."

Of course, she's obviously a troubled young lady and we don't know her entire story, but we do know that so many more black women are legitimately abused, exploited, and raped, and are dismissed and disbelieved. And while it is tragic that the young white male lacrosse players were officially unfairly charged, there is by no means a parallel in their circumstance and that of the Rutgers players. The Duke players were at a raucous party they organized with young black women as featured strippers, reinforcing the subordinate position of black females within a white patriarchal worldview, while the Rutgers players were on the court of athletic excellence performing at the top of their sport.

Peterson: I have a beautiful daughter and son. It is painfully clear to me after watching the splendid young ladies from the Rutgers basketball team respond to the attack on their integrity by Imus that, although black men should pay serious attention to the plight of young black males, we should pay equal attention to the plight of our daughters and young females as well. Do you agree?

Dyson: Absolutely. Over the past twenty years, there has been a great deal of concern about the crisis of young black males: their alarming rates of incarceration, their poor schooling, their social stigma, and their death at the hands of police or another brother. While such attention to our sons is wholly warranted, black folk haven't dedicated nearly as much energy to the plight of black girls. Our daughters have often suffered silently; too often, their need for social support and communal investment has slid quietly off the racial radar. Great psychic harm is done to black girls when they absorb the message that their lives don't count as much as their brothers' or their uncles'.

But the opposite is just as true: young black girls who feel the love of their parents are able to overcome huge obstacles in forging a healthy sense of self. Black daughters who know beyond the shadow of a doubt that their daddy loves and adores them tap a source of confidence that the world can't quench. We have heard the stories of woe and absence; we have borne painful witness a thousand times over to black men who scatter seeds in vulnerable wombs only to abandon them before they are properly nourished. But there are other stories too: tales of faithful devotion to the care and protection of adolescent ladies; narratives of nurture in the midnight hour of diaper changes when mothers are fast asleep; and reports of first dates with daddy onboard to make sure that baby girl won't be hoodwinked or bamboozled by a fast-talking replica of his younger, irresponsible self.

While good black fathers are far more plentiful than either the media or warped social science would have us believe, their far-reaching effect can't be adequately calculated in journalistic accounts, or in cold statistics or flat analysis. The moral beauty of a black father's determined embrace of his female offspring pays off in startling dividends: she won't feel the need to lay with the first guy who is smooth and seductive; she is less likely to be sidetracked by a nagging lack of confidence that often takes hold of those without strong male support; and she won't permit the adamant naysayer to rain on her personal or professional parade. The advantages don't end there. She'll take far more chances in her choice of work or play; she'll see beyond the provincial thinking that hampers women in sexist worldviews; and she'll beam with inner pride in her accomplishments even when insecure peers or lovers mock her ambition.

Peterson: Finally, do you think the Imus affair has high-lighted the intense gender crisis at the heart of a great deal of rap music that may give greater weight to Nas's claim that hip hop is dead?

Dyson: Yes I do. When Nas uttered the words "hip hop is dead," he joined a long list of prophets and fed-up practitioners who've announced the death of a field, only to jump-start a new phase of its growth. Author V. S. Naipaul declared the novel dead, then went on to win the Nobel Prize in literature for his highly regarded fiction. Philosopher Richard Rorty declared that philosophy was dead in 1979, and even though he no longer teaches in philosophy departments, he has continued to publish lively philosophical books. And let's not forget, Nas announced hip hop's death on a hip hop album!

Of course, if you've got no sense of humor, or if you're stuck on literalism, then you can't really appreciate what Nas and those who support his claim are up to. Hip hop as a commercial enterprise is surely full of death. Great rhetoric has lost its sway as noble verbal art has been replaced by the mindless redundancy of themes we're all too familiar with: women, weed, wine, cars, and jewelry. The thug persona has replaced skillful exploration of the thug's predicament: hustling in a culture where crime is the only option of the economically vulnerable. Beyond questions of craft, there's the archetypical rap record executive who's more interested in releasing records by artists reveling in rims rather than rhymes, and in breasts and behinds more than setting young brains on fire with knowledge of their people's plight. Of course, the culture at large is more enthusiastic about *Pimp My Ride* than *Nightline*.

In a sense, the "hip hop is dead" movement is responding to an ancient problem: the masses seem to be attracted to producers of the lowest-quality entertainment while the makers of superior art suffer by comparison. When Jay-Z released his classic first album *Reasonable Doubt*, universally praised for its lyrical inventiveness, he admitted later on wax that "I gave you prophecy on my first joint but y'all lamed out / didn't really appreciate it 'til the second one came out." Of course, when Jay-Z became a commercial monster, he was criticized for his extravagant materialism. And Nas's widely celebrated first offering, the monumental *Illmatic*, took longer than it should have to go gold. But when he made more commercially viable music, he too came in for a critical drubbing. Nas seems to have this in mind when he laments on his latest album that "I can't sound smart 'cause y'all will run away." In short, the street runs both ways: beyond the crass machinations of corporate executives who are ruining hip hop's "street ghetto essence," we sometimes get the artists we deserve, or are taught to crave. If we could more readily appreciate artists' true lyrical greatness, maybe we'd demand a lot more of it and reward it and support it when it came along.

Nas is absolutely right to hold hip hop's feet to his rhetorical fire. Hearing Nas spew his righteous venom is like hearing a god of hip hop prophesy to his corrupt and corroded culture. With the exception of some artists and label stars, the masses of black folk who should have a larger financial stake in the commercial core of the culture have been all but banned from its profits. There is mindless aping of sounds and concepts that sell. Politically conscious and progressive hip hop artists are nearly invisible and inaudible on radio and music video television. And the sheer elegance of hip hop craft, tailored by artists with the highest regard for verbal dexterity and lyrical innovation, is crushed under the juggernaut of minstrelsy and the numbing glorification of guns, gluteuses, and grills.

But lest those outside the culture kick dirt on the coffin of hip hop too quickly, they should be reminded that most didn't bother to support hip hop when political consciousness was au courant back in the late 1980s and early 1990s. Most naysayers didn't bother to commercially or intellectually support the folk they thought were on point, and judging by the record sales of contemporary conscious rappers, not much has changed. Such hypocrisy is reason enough to call off the dogs and have a broader conversation about hip hop's future.

The most powerful sign that hip hop *culture* is alive, and desperate to breathe, is that it has launched such a withering critique from *within* about the industry that houses it—or makes it homeless, as it were. Where is the parallel and public critique in the black church, where patriarchy and bling reign in the gospel of prosperity with greater ugliness than in hip hop? (After all, Diddy didn't claim to be called, just a shot caller). Hip hop is vital precisely because it is able to take stock and grow up and look back and move forward. Hip hop is alive because two of its greatest MCs ever, Jay-Z and Nas, on their latest albums wrestle in grown-up fashion with the plagues on its cultural house. And don't forget to listen to Nas's last song on the album *Hip Hop Is Dead:* "Hope," where he declares, a capella, that "Hip hop will never, never die." Horrible hip hop, the kind that revels in the exploitation and demonization of women, must die so that regal hip hop can live. Hip hop is dead. Long live hip hop.

OUTRO

by Nas

It's brothers like Michael Eric Dyson who can give CPR to hip hop. The pulse may be weak and the breathing may be shallow, but it's brothers like Michael Eric Dyson who can get that heart to beat again. The sirens may be drawing nearer by the second, and the afternoon's industrial haze may predict a dark night, but it's warriors like Michael Eric Dyson who can make sure that hip hop sees another dawn. It's warriors like Michael Eric Dyson who can make sure that hip hop doesn't stay dead forever.

Michael Eric Dyson can give hip hop a future by making us hold tight to the strength of our past and by making apparent the promise of our present. Year after year, in book after book, Professor Dyson has written eloquently about the history of African American people and paid special attention to the importance of hip hop music in that experience. He reminds us where we came from, and he tells us that what we do can be so crucial. In his own life he saw all around him how easily straight steps can run crooked, and how injustice can find you, even in the house of the Lord.

He has taken up the pen as his weapon of choice while others settle for less noble instruments. He has set down the story from our point of view. Michael Eric Dyson writes and speaks with the same lyrical skill and rhetorical brilliance that we praise in the greatest MCs. I've seen this man verbally battle archconservative Bill O'Reilly on the Fox News network, dropping lines of inspired poetry about black perseverance and possibility to an audience that is most comfortable watching a black man on a surveillance camera. He has spoken before elected officials and defended my craft. With his irrepressible intelligence, Professor Dyson battles at the lectern rather than in the nightclub, and the world is better for it.

He embraces hip hop in all of its forms. He embraces the troubles and missteps just as freely as he does the visionary genius of artists like Biggie and Pac. His point of view reminds us that there was a time when hip hop music was at the edge. We were once the avant-garde. In New York we came from the Outer Boroughs and in every sense all across the country—North, South, East, and West. We all came from the fringes to take hold of the mainstream. And we all stood together overlooking that precipice of urban disaster and moral decay. Back then, there were no systems in place, no A&R talent scouts poking around Queensbridge, no critics in the newspapers talking about our rhymes or our battles, no focus groups of suburban teenagers being sequestered in skyscrapers on Madison Avenue.

Now we've forgotten our past. We've forgotten our genesis. And we suffer for this loss. People only remember what slot your album got on the Billboard Top 100, or how many stars your album got in some magazine review. The past has been processed and homogenized for mass consumption. When the machine got real big, real fast, those pioneers like Marley Marl and Rakim weren't in the background any longer. People on both sides of the record sleeve have forgotten why we do what we do.

When you see black faces being whitewashed in history textbooks, and white faces making black music on MTV and BET, it becomes even easier to forget the jump off point for all of this. Too many people are content to sit home night after night watching the latest network television minstrel sitcom because they don't know where this nonsense came from. No movement can thrive if it doesn't recall its birth. We need to be able to learn from our history if we are going to take control of our future. Not only has Michael Eric Dyson shown us this truth, but he has shown us that it is possible. He has risen through the ranks of educated men and made his voice heard. We should all listen to what he says, and what he writes, because in his words we will find the tools to build ourselves and hip hop back up.

Some folks got angry when I told them that hip hop is dead. Other folks got confused when I told them that hip hop is dead. Still others knew that I was right. People disagreed and spilled ink on magazine pages freely like cheap wine or young blood to argue with each other and with me. Although the voices may have clashed, the one constant in the clamor was that all of these people out there felt that hip hop was worth fighting over and fighting for.

I agree because I love hip hop, and I am glad that Michael Eric Dyson is on our side.

Know what I mean?

SPECIAL THANKS

I want to thank the following people and institutions for their contributions to this concept album of a book: Jay-Z (mad thanks for the intro); Nas (mad thanks for the outro); the late Liz Maguire (miss and love you); Chris Greenberg (who did yeoman's work in shaping and supporting the product you hold in your hand); Amy Scheibe; Nicole Caputo (beautiful cover); Christine Marra; Chrisona Schmidt; *Callaloo* and *That's the Joint* for allowing me to express some of these words first in their pages; *Ebony*, Rachel Vassel, and Eve Ensler for allowing me to use my words in their venues in my gender remix; James Peterson; Meta DuEwa Jones; Thomas Gibson; Byron Hurt; Marc Hill (whose dissertation I signed and helped direct); Paul Farber; the hip hop radio shows across the country, especially Philadelphia's 100.3 *Morning Show*, featuring Monie, Pooch, and Laiya, with Izzo in the streets; my crew—Susan "Queen" Taylor and Khephra "Smooth" Burns and Stanley "Captain" Perkins and

Barbara Perkins and Karen Lloyd and Linda Johnson Rice and Mel Farr ("Superstar") and Marc Morial and Michelle Miller and Andriette Earl and Kashka and Horace Mansfield and Yolanda Mansfield and D. Soyini Madison; and to my family—Addie Mae Dyson (happy 70th birthday, Mama); Anthony Dyson; Everett Dyson (hang in there, man); Gregory Dyson; Brian Dyson; Michael Eric Dyson II (congratulations and thank-you Jesus on graduating from Morehouse!); Mwata Dyson, M.D.; Maisha Daniels; Ray Daniels; and Rev. Marcia L. Dyson (thanks for the love and support).

INDEX

ABOUT THE AUTHOR

Michael Eric Dyson has been named by *Ebony* as one of the hundred most influential black Americans, and is the author of fourteen other books, including *Come Hell or High Water*. Dyson is University Professor at Georgetown University, where he teaches Theology, English, and African American Studies.